Hippie, Inc.

the misunderstood subculture that
changed the way we live and generated
billions of dollars in the process

Hippie, Inc.

Michael Klassen

SixOneSeven Books

Permissions requests may be addressed to
SixOneSeven Books
21 Wormwood Street
Ste. 325
Boston, MA 02210
www.sixonesevenbooks.com

Grateful acknowledgment is made to the following for permission to quote from copyrighted material:

Burton H. Wolfe, *The Hippies* (Signet, 1968)
Fred Turner, *From Counterculture to Cyberculture* (The University of Chicago Press, 2006)
Ken Kesey, *One Flew Over The Cuckoo's Nest* (Penguin Random House, 1962)
Walter Isaacson, *Steve Jobs* (Simon & Schuster, 2011)

Boston / Michael Klassen—First Edition
ISBN 978-0-9831505-6-5

Printed in the United States of America

CONTENTS

PART V: ORIGINALS

APPENDICES

NEIGHBORHOOD

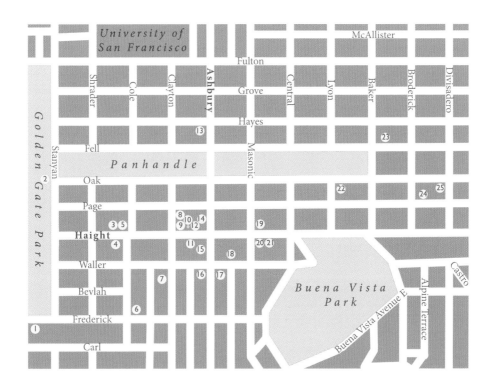

THE ORIGINAL HIPPIE SCENE

(residents, workers, frequent visitors)*

1. ABIGAIL FOLGER 2. ADELE BONOVITZ 3. AL KRAMER 4. AL LIGHT 5. AL NEIMAN 6. AL RINKER 7. ALEC TSONGAS 8. ALEX GELUARDI 9. ALEX WEISS 10. ALLAN WATTS 11. (DR.) ALLEN CLARK D.D.S. 12. ALLEN COHEN 13. ALLEN GINSBERG 14. ALLEN KATZMAN 15. ALLEN MICHAEL 16. ALLEN MYERSON 17. ALLEN NOONAN 18. ALLEN SCHMER 19. ALTON KELLEY 20. AMBROSE HOLLINGSWORTH 21. AMI MAGILL 22. ANNA HALPRIN 23. ANNE EDMAN NÉE PORTEUS 24. ANNE WATERUD 25. ANTON LAVEY 26. ANTONIO PINEDA 27. APACHE 28. APRIL SHOWER 29. ARLO ACTON 30. ARNOLD 31. ART KUNKIN 32. ARTHUR LISCH 33. ARTHUR MONROE 34. ASHOKE FAKIR 35. AUGUSTUS OWSLEY STANLEY, III (A.K.A. OWSLEY) 36. AUNT ELLEN 37. AVRIL WEBER 38. AVRUM RUBENSTEIN 39. B.J. PAPA 40. BARBARA 41. BARON WOLMAN 42. BARRY MELTON 43. BEN JACOPETTI 44. BEN NIEVES 45. BEN VAN METER 46. BESS FARR 47. BIG BLACK 48. BIG JOHN 49. BILBO 50. BILL FORTNER 51. BILL FRITSCH (A.K.A SWEET WILLIAM) 52. BILL GRAHAM 53. BILL HAM 54. BILL KELLY 55. BILL LINDEN 56. BILL LOUGHSBOROUGH 57. BILL MASON 58. BILL REZNER 59. (DR.) BILL ROBBINS, D.D.S. 60. BILL SMITH 61. BILL THOMPSON 62. BILL WEER 63. BILL WHEELER 64. BILLY HITCHCOCK 65. BILLY KREUTZMAN 66. BILLY LANDOUT 67. BILLY MURCOTT 68. BOB BRANNIMAN 69. BOB CUFF 70. BOB FRIED 71. BOB SCHNEPF 72. BOB SEIDEMANN 73. BOB SIMON 74. BOB STUBBS 75. BOBBIE BROWN 76. BOB KAUFMAN 77. BOBBY BEAUSOLEIL 78. BOBBY BOWLES 79. BOBBY COLLINS 80. BOBBY HUTCHERSON 81. BOBBY WEIR 82. BOBSIE 83. BONNIE BEECHER (A.K.A. JAHANARA ROMNEY) 84. BONNIE MACLEAN 85. BOOTS HUSTON 86. BOZ SCAGGS 87. BRIAN EDMAN 88. BRIAN ROHAN 89. BRUCE BRUGGMAN 90. BRUCE CONNER 91. BRUCE DAUSER 92. BUBBA FREE JOHN 93. BUD 94. BUDDHA 95. BURT KANEGSON 96. BURTON H. WOLFE 97. BUTCHER BROOKS 98. CACTUS FLOWER 99. CAITLIN WILLIAMS 100. CARL HIRSCH 101. CARLOS SANTANA 102. CARMELLA 103. CAROL HINTON 104. CAROL KESSLER 105. CAROLYN ADAMS (A.K.A. MOUNTAIN GIRL) 106. CARRIE CLAUSEN 107. CARRIE NATION 108. CHANDLER LAUGHLIN, III 109. CHANITA 110. CHARLENE ALLREAD 111. CHARLES HALL 112. CHARLES MANSON 113. CHARLES PERRY 114. CHARLIE ARTMAN (A.K.A. CHARLIE BROWN) 115. CHARLIE PLYMEL 116. CHARLOTTE TODD 117. CHERYL FAHNER 118. CHERYL WHITE 119. CHESTER ANDERSON 120. CHESTER A. ARTHUR 121. CHET HELMS 122. CHICKIE P. GARBANZA 123. CHLOE FERGUSON 124. CHOCOLATE GEORGE 125. CHRIS ROBINSON 126. CHRISTINE PARA 127. CHRISTOPHER TREE 128. CHUCK JONES 129. CHUCK STEAKS 130. CINDY MORTON 131. CINDY SMALL 132. CLAUDE HAYWARD 133. CLAYTON LEWIS 134. CLIFF ROBERTSON 135. CLOUDBURST 136. CRAIG MORTON 137. CRICKY DICK 138. CUPID 139. CURLY JIM 140. DAN BRUHNS 141. DAN HICKS 142. DANA CRUMB 143. DANGERFIELD ASHTON 144. DANNY RIFKIN 145. DARBY SLICK 146. DARCI 147. DARIC 148. DAVE GETZ 149. DAVE NELSON 150. DAVE ROTHKOP 151. DAVE TORBERT 152. DAVID BAAR 153. DAVID BOROUGH 154. DAVID BYRD 155. DAVID FRIEBERG 156. DAVID HARRIS 157. DAVID LAFLAMME 158. DAVID LEBRUN 159. DAVID LICKERT 160. DAVID MELTZER 162. DAVID RICHARDS 163. (DR.) DAVID SMITH, M.D. 164. DAVID SIMPSON 165. DAVID SINGER 166. DAVY COFFIN 167. DEBORAH WOLF 168. DEL CLOSE 169. DELANO DEAN 170. DENIE NOLAN 171. DENNIS LONG 172. DENNY ZEITLIN 173. DEWEY REDMAN 174. DICK BURGESS (A.K.A., SGT. SUNSHINE) 175. DICKIE PETERSON 176. DINO VALENTI 177. DON BUCHLA 178. DON COCHRAN 179. DON CROW 180. DON HUTTON 181. DON SCHENKER 182. DON STEVENS 183. DONNA CHABAM-DELMAS 184. DONNAKOVA DAUSER 185. DOTTIE IVORY 186. DWIGHT SIMS 187. EARL BLUE 188. ED DENSON 189. ED HARRIS 190. ED McCLANAHAN 191. EDMOND SHEA 192. ELBERT ROBINSON (A.K.A. JUBA) 193. ELENA SCOVIL 194. ELIAS ROMERO 195. ELIZABETH (BETTY) GIBBS 196. ELIZABETH SANCHEZ 197. ELLEN HARMON 198. ELLEN KAUFMAN 199. ELVIN BISHOP 200. EMMETT GROGAN 201. ERIC ALBRONDA 202. ERIC BERNE 203. ERIC CHRISTENSEN 204. ERIC NORD (A.K.A. "BIG DADDY" ERIC NORD) 205. ERIC WATERUD 206. ERIK WEBER 207. ESTHER HOLLINGSWORTH 208. ESTHER HARTSHORN 209. ESTHER SEALUND 210. (DR.) EUGENE SCHOENFELD, M.D—A.K.A. DR. HIPPOCRATES 211. EVA BESSIE 212. FAITH PETRIC 213. FAMOUS MELISSA 214. FELICIA 215. FISH THE QUAKER 216. (DR.) FRANCIS RIGNEY 217. FRANK 218. FRANK CIECIORKA 219. FRANK WERBER 220. FRED 221. FRED ROHE 222. FREDDIE KUH 223. FREEWHEELIN' FRANK 224. FRIDA 225. FRNKA 226. FYLLIS 227. GABE KATZ 228. GAIL THOMAS 229. GANDALF 230. GARY DUNCAN 231. GARY EDSON ARLINGTON 232. GARY GOLDHILL 233. GARY GOODROW 234. GARY SNYDER 235. GAVIN ARTHUR 236. GENE ANTHONY 237. GENE ESTERBU 238. GENE GRIMM 239. GEORGE B. LEONARD 240. GEORGE CONGER 241. GEORGE HUNTER 242. GEORGE McCLURE 243. GEORGE MONTANA 244. GEORGE TSONGAS 245. GERALD ROSEN 246. GERD STERN 247. GERHARDT NICHOLSON 248. GILBERT SHELTON 249. GINNY GOOD 250. GIRL FRIEBERG 251. GLEN McKAY 252. GLORIA ROBERTSON 253. GRACE SLICK 254. GRAHAM MACKINTOSH 255. GRAHAM NASH 256. GRANT JACOBS 257. GREG ELMORE 258. GREG IRONS 259. GURNEY NORMAN 260. GUT 261. HADLEY CALIMAN 262. HAL WAGENET 263. HALDON CHASE 264. HAMILTON CAMP 265. HANK HARRISON 266. HANNAH STILLS 267. HARRY MONROE 268. HARVEY KORNSPAN 269. HARVEY MANDEL 270. HEIDI McGURRIN 271. HENRY KOT 272. HERB CAEN 273. HERB GREENE 274. HERBERT BLAU 275. HETTI McGEE 276. HILLEL REZNER 277. HONEY GREEN 278. HOWARD REINGOLD 279. HOWIE MINKIN 280. HUGH ROMNEY (A.K.A.WAVY GRAVY) 281. HYLA DEER (A.K.A. HYLA STRAUCH, HYLA DAVIDOVICH) 282. IDA ZINNS 283. INA MAE GASKIN 284. IRENE SCHENKER 285. IRVING FROMER 286. J. TONY SERRA 287. JACK CASADY 288. JACK JACKSON (A.K.A., JAXON) 289. JACK LEVINE 290. JACK WEINBERG 291. JAMES BRAUGHTON 292. JAMES COOKE 293. JAMES E. WHITE 294. JAMES GURLEY 295. JAMES MELCHERT 296. JAMIE 297. JAN BLUE 298. JANE BURTON 299. JANE LAPINER 300. JANIS JOPLIN 301. JAY 302. JAY THELIN 303. JEAN PAUL PICKENS 304. JEANNE ROSE 305. JEFFERY KESSLER (A.K.A., HIRAM STRAIGHT) 306. JENNY HUNTER 307. JEROME ARNOLD 308. JERRY GARCIA 309. JERRY KAMSTRA 310. JERRY MANDER 311. JERRY SEALUND (A.K.A. BLIND JERRY) 312. JERRY SLICK 313. JERRY WELCH 314. JESSE FOSTER 315. JIM EDMAN 316. JIM GUYETTE 317. JIM HAYNIE 318. JIM MARSHALL 319. JIM MORRISON 320. JIM MURRAY 321. JIM PETERMAN 322. JIM QUESKIN 323. JIMI SIEGEL 324. JOAN BROWN 325. JOANNA BROWNSON 326. JOANNE BAGEN 327. JOANNE KYGER 328. JODI PALLADINI (A.K.A. LUNA MOTH) 329. JOE GOMEZ 330. JOE LIZOWSKI 331. JOE McDONALD (A.K.A. COUNTRY JOE) 332. JOEL 333. JOEL BECK 334. JOEL ROBERTS 335. JOEY COVINGTON 336. JOHN ALIOTO 337. JOHN BROWNE 338. JOHN BROWNSON 339. JOHN CARPENTER 340. JOHN CIPOLLINA 341. JOHN FAHEY 342. JOHN FROMER 343. JOHN GREGORY 344. JOHN HADLEY 345. JOHN HANDY 346. JOHN-JOHN 347. JOHN KORNFIELD 348. JOHN LUBY 349. JOHN

PAGE BROWNING 350. JOHN THE CHEMIST 351. JOHN WHITE 352. JOHN WONG 353. JOHNNIE HELMS 354. JOHNNY WALKER 355. JON HENDRICKS 356. JONI BRANSTTEN 357. JORMA KAUKONEN 358. JOYCE FRANCISCO 359. JUDITH GOLDHAFT 360. JUDITH PEARLMAN 361. JUDY BLUE 362. JUDY COHON 363. JUDY DUGGAN 364. JULIUS KARPEN 365. KAREN 366. KASHA 367. KAT 368. KATHI MCDONALD 369. KATHRYN ISH 370. KATHRYN SHIRLEY 371. KEITH ABRAMS 372. KEITH JARRETT 373. KEN BABBS 374. KEN GOLDFINGER (A.K.A. KEN CONNELL) 375. KEN KESEY 376. KEN RAND 377. KENNETH ANGER 378. KENNETH PATCHEN 379. KENNETH REXROTH 380. KENT MINAULT 381. KIRBY DOYLE 382. KNUTE STILES 383. KURT BANKS 384. LA MORTADELLA 385. LAIRD GRANT 386. LARRY BENNETT 387. LARRY HANKIN 388. LARRY JORDAN 389. LARRY WEST 390. LATIF HARRIS 391. LAUREL BURCH 392. LAURIE 393. LAVAL 394. LEE CONKLIN 395. LEE MICHAELS 396. LEIGH STEPHENS 397. LENNIE SCHEFTMAN 398. LENNIE SILVERBERG 399. LENNY BRUCE 400. LENNY HOROWITZ 401. LENORE KANDEL 402. LEON HARRIS (A.K.A., FATHER LEON HARRIS) 403. (DR.) LEON TABORY 404. LEONARD NATHAN 405. LEONARD WOLF 406. LESLIE BRILLIANT 407. LESLIE CORRELL 408. LESLIE KAMSTRA 409. LESLIE WEST 410. LEWIS RAPPAPORT 411. LINDA 412. LINDA LAFLAMME 413. LINDA TILLERY 414. LISA LAW 415. LITTLE ROBERT 416. LITTLE WOLF 417. LONNIE TURNER 418. LORD BUCKLEY 419. LORIN GILLETTE 420. LOU GOTTLEIB 421. LOUIS "LEFTY" GONZALES 422. LOUIS CISCO 423. LUCINDA 424. LUCY LEWIS 425. LURIA CASTELL 426. LUTHER GREEN 427. LYDIA PENSE 428. MAC MCGREW 429. MAGGIE GASKIN 430. MAGIC MARCO 431. MALACHI 432. MARCIA LICKERT 433. MARCIE BENDRELL-TARDELL 434. MARGO ST. JAMES 435. MARI TEPPER 436. MARILYN HARRIS 437. MARK BRAUNSTEIN 438. MARK LINENTHAL 439. MARK MCLOUD 440. MARK NAFTALIN 441. MARK RYAN 442. MARK UNOBSKY 443. MARMADUKE 444. MARSHA THELIN 445. MARSHALL MACLUHAN 446. MARTA 447. MARTINE 448. MARTINE BOWEN 449. MARTY BALIN 450. MARTY JACOBS 451. MARVIN LIPOFSKY 452. MARY COROT 453. MARY KORTA (A.K.A., SISTER MARY KORTA) 454. MATTHEW KATZ 455. MAX SCHERR 456. MAYNE SMITH 457. MERIMEE MOFFITT 458. MERRY 459. MICHAEL BOWEN 460. MICHAEL CALLAHAN 461. MICHAEL CUBERSTON 462. MICHAEL FERGUSON 463. MICHAEL FLAUTT 464. MICHAEL FRIMKIS 465. MICHAEL KOSMAN 466. MICHAEL LEFFERT 467. MICHAEL LEWIS 468. MICHAEL MCCLURE 469. MICHAEL STEPANIAN 470. MICHAEL THOMAS 471. MICKEY HART 472. MIKE BLOOMFIELD 473. MIKE FERGUSON 474. MIKE HAGEN 475. MIKE KARBO 476. MIKE KEEGAN 477. MIKE RUSH 478. MIKE WILHELM 479. MIMI FARINA NÉE BAEZ 480. MOE MOSKOWITZ 481. MONICA COLLIER 482. MORNING GLORY 483. MORT WOLF, D.V.M. 484. MORTON SUBOTNICK 485. MOTORCYCLE RITCHIE 486. NANCY GETZ 487. NANCY GURLEY 488. NANCY VAN BRASCH HAMREN 489. NATASHA 490. NATURAL SUZAN 491. NEAL CASSADY 492. NEIL YOUNG 493. NICK GRAVENITES 494. NICK OLGILVIE 495. NICKY HOPKINS 496. NINA BLASENHEIM (A.K.A. NANANINA) 497. NOEL 498. NORMA HAXBY (A.K.A. FAYE HAXBY, FAYE KESEY) 499. NORMAN STUBBS 500. OPHIEL STREET 501. PAGE BROWNING 502. PAMELA 503. PANCHO 504. PARRIE 505. PASSIONFLOWER 506. PAT 507. PATRICK GLEESON 508. PATRUSHKA 509. PAUL BASSETT 510. PAUL BUTTERFIELD 511. PAUL FOSTER 512. PAUL KANTNER 513. PAUL KRASSNER 514. PAULA MCCOY 515. PAULA SUNDSTREN 516. PEGGY CASSERTA 517. PENELOPE DEVRIES 518. PENNIE CULBERSTON 519. PETER ALBIN 520. PETER BAILEY 521. PETER BERG 522. PETER COYOTE (A.K.A., PETER COHON) 523. PETER KRAMER 524. PETER KRUG 525. PETER MACKANESS 526. PETER MASON BOND 527. PETER ORLOVSKY 528. PETER VOULKOS 529. PHIL HAMMOND 530. PHIL LESH 531. PHIL NORMAND 532. PHYLLIS WILLNER 533. PIERRE DE LATTRE (A.K.A. FATHER PIERRE DE LATTRE) 534. R. CRUMB 535. RABBI DAVID 536. RAFAEL GARRETT 537. RAINBIRD 538. RAINBOW 539. RAINDROP 540. RALPH ABRAHAM 541. RALPH ACKERMAN 542. RALPH METZNER 543. RAMON SENDER 544. RANDY SALAS 545. RANDY TUTEN 546. RAY ANDERSEN 547. RAY GIRAURD 548. REGGIE WILLIAMS 549. RENE RAMIREZ 550. RENEE SHEDROFF 551. RENN 552. REV. BILL BIGELOW 553. REV. JEFFERSON FUCK POLAND 554. RHEA 555. RICHARD 556. RICHARD ALPERT (A.K.A. BABA RAM DAS) 557. RICHARD BAKER 558. RICHARD BLUE 559. RICHARD BRAUTIGAN 560. RICHARD CORRELL 561. RICHARD ELLMAN 562. RICHARD FAHRNER 563. RICHARD FARINA 564. RICHARD PRICE 565. RICHARD STAFFORD 566. RICHARD STAHL 567. RICHARD WHITE 568. RICHIE KESSSLER 569. RICHIE OLSEN 570. RICK GRIFFIN 571. RICK TURNER 572. RITA WEILL 573. ROBBIE BASHO 574. ROBERT BAKER 575. ROBERT BURCH 576. ROBERT COLLINS 577. ROBERT EASLEY 578. ROBERT FRIED 579. ROBERT HUNTER 580. ROBERT LIMON 581. ROBERT TREE 582. ROBERTO LA MORTICELLA 583. ROBIN 584. ROBIN MCGILL 585. ROCHELLE RAMIREZ 586. ROCK SCULLY 587. RODNEY ALBIN 588. ROGER HILLYARD 589. ROLAND HANNA 590. RON BEVIRT (A.K.A. HASSLER) 591. RON BOISE 592. RON LAFOND 593. RON MCKERNAN (A.K.A. PIGPEN) 594. RON NAGLE 595. RON STALLINGS 596. RON THELIN 597. RON TURNER 598. RON WICKERSHAMM 599. RONNIE DAVIS 600. RONNY GOLDMAN 601. RONNY FULLER 602. ROSEANNE FOREST 603. RUTH WEISS 604. S. CLAY WILSON 605. S. PAUL GEE 606. SAM ANDREW 607. SAM LAY 608. SAMUEL L. LEWIS (A.K.A. SUFI SAM) 609. (DR.) SANDOR BURSTEIN M.D. 610. SANDRA BUTLER 611. SANDY ARCHER 612. SANDY BULL 613. SANDY GIMPLE 614. SANDY LEHMAN-HAUPT 615. SARA ESTERBU 616. SARA WEER 617. SASHA 618. SATTY 619. SCHLOMO CARLEBACH (A.K.A. THE "SINGING RABBI") 620. SCOTT BEACH 621. SCOTTIE MCCLEAN 622. SHARON GIMPLE 623. SHAUNA POPE 624. SHERRI 625. SHIRLEY WISE 626. SIGNE HASSO ANDERSON 627. SIMOLEAN GARY 628. SKIP OLSEN 629. SLIM MINNAUX 630. SONJA MAGILL 631. SONNY SIMMONS 632. SPADE JOHNNIE 633. SPAIN RODRIGUEZ 634. SPENCER DRYDEN 635. STACEY 636. STANLEY J. MILLER, JR. (A.K.A. STANLEY MOUSE) 637. STANLEY MCDANIEL 638. STEPHANIE SUNSHINE 639. DR. STERLING BUNELL M.D. 640. STEVE COHEN 641. STEVE GASKIN 642. STEVE LAMBRECHT 643. STEVE LEIPER 644. STEVE LEVINE 645. STEVE MILLER 646. STEVE MORK (A.K.A. MORK) 647. STEVE WHITE 648. STEVEN ARNOLD 649. STEVEN KROLICK 650. STEWART BRAND 651. STORM CLOUD 652. SUE ALSEN 653. SUPER SPADE 654. SUSAN KESSLER 655. SUSAN GOOD 656. SUSAN VAN METER 657. SUSIE ALLREAD 658. SUSIE WACKER 659. SUZUKI ROSHIN 660. SY LOWINSKY 661. TALL PAUL 662. TAMBOO 663. TAMMY HARTSHORN (A.K.A. HELENA LEBRUN) 664. TANGERINE 665. TERESA MURPHY 666. TERRÉ 667. TERRENCE HALLINAN 668. TERRY RILEY 669. THOMAS ALGERNON WEIR 670. THOMAS KOENIG 671. TIGGER 672. TIM DAVIS 673. TIM SCULLY 674. TIMOTHY LEARY 675. TOBACCO 676. TOM CONSTANTEN 677. TOM DEWITT 678. TOM DONOHUE (A.K.A. TOM "BIG DADDY" DONOHUE) 679. TOM WOLFE 680. TONY MARTIN 681. TOOK 682. TOSH 683. TRAVIS RIVERS 684. TREEBEARD 685. TSVI STRAUCH (A.K.A., HARRY STRAUCH, TSVI DEER) 686. TUMBLEWEED 687. TURKEY 688. TWEEDLEDEE 689. TWEEDLEDUM 690. VICKI POLLACK 691. VICTOR GRANT 692. VICTOR MOSCOSO 693. VINCE 694. VINCE DALVISO 695. VIRGINIA WOOLF 696. WALLY HEDRICK 697. WES WILSON 698. WILHELM JOERRES 699. WILLOWHERB 700. WOODY FLOYD 701. YANA CROW 702. YOPGIS 703. YURI TOROPOV 704. YVONNE RAND 705. ZACK STEWART

*APOLOGIES FOR ANYONE LEFT OUT OR MISTAKENLY PUT IN

INTRODUCTION

The Haight-Ashbury community really worked well in the beginning.
There was a lot of love, good vibes, dancing and a real feel of community. As the media paid more and more attention to the Haight and
started calling us Hippies the word spread across America and thousands of kids decided to make the trek to San Francisco. We tried to
prepare the City for the influx and conjured up the "Summer of Love" as
a way to encourage cooperation and concern about the vast numbers of
young people that were going to arrive. The City, the police and the
hip community needed to work together but all of our pleas were in
vain. This was the beginning of the end for the hippie community.

—*Jay Thelin*

Haight Street in mid-summer 1967 was a nightmare. Alcoholics, pick-
pockets, thieves, con men, drug addicts, sex degenerates, and knifers
roamed the area through the night and early morning hours.

—*Burton H. Wolfe,* The Hippies

O N THE AFTERNOON of October 6th, 1967 in the increasingly notorious San Francisco community popularly known as
"Haight-Ashbury," the Diggers, a street theater group, held a mock
funeral march mourning the death of the hippies. Over the previous two
years, the neighborhood had deteriorated, riddled with drugs and crime and

venereal disease. What had begun as an optimistic journey of discovery was devolving into a hellhole.

The original hippies had been looking to create a freer, and more authentic community, more in touch with the natural as opposed to the plastic. They wanted a society where people could shape their lives on their own terms and live harmoniously with each other and the planet. The later hippies, the runaways, posers, and impostors, were not always grounded in those values.

Despite the demise of Haight-Ashbury, many of the original hippies continued to live by their values. Some stayed in the Haight. Others moved to rural communes and others left hippiedom to transform themselves into successful artists, executives, entrepreneurs, and environmental activists.

The funeral march, reflecting the disappointment and disgust of some of the original hippies, left a shroud over the legacy of this counter-culture, obscuring some of its great accomplishments. In retrospect, we know that the funeral marked the demise of the original hippie movement, but not the end of the many innovative products and ideas that sprung from the minds of its leaders, nor did it stop the expanding influence of the beliefs and products that the hippies popularized. The original hippies' remarkable success story is the focus of this book.

The idea for *Hippie, inc.,* first came to me one fall day in 2007. My wife and I were seeing our younger son off to college in Santa Barbara, California. We were walking down State Street, the city's upscale retail district, which runs the gamut from locally owned surf shops to Tiffany's, when a place called The Peace Store caught my eye. Curiosity drew me inside. The Peace Store turned out to be a cleaned-up, expensive version of the standard sixties head shop, with the usual hippie paraphernalia ranging from peace sign key chains ($6) to "Summer 66" distressed jeans ($89) to tie-dyed duvet covers ($175). The colorful merchandise was displayed neatly on shelves and racks between spacious aisles, beneath a ceiling two stories high. The walls were covered with John Lennon sayings and psychedelic graffiti, but there was no grime, no aroma of pot, not even any bongs for sale. As a professor of business at the University of Northern Iowa, specializing in advertising, consumer behavior, and the principles of marketing, I immediately asked myself: "How can a shop that sells nothing but 'hippie stuff' stay afloat in a commercial zone where monthly rent must run as high as $25,000?"

Haight Street

Corner of
Haight and
Ashbury

Early Arrivals:
Summer of Love

That first question led me to others, to wonder more generally what the hippies had created commercially and what, if anything, hippie-initiated enterprises might be worth today. What could my business students learn from the hippies? What could all of the young entrepreneurs and small businesses, marketing themselves, branding themselves in the modern Internet world learn from this subculture of the 1960s? The pursuit of answers to those questions led me on a fascinating eight-year quest. The more I've learned the more excited and impressed I've become by the hippies' legacy.

Business people understand that their success depends not on outstanding ideas or even great products, but on *demand*. Consumers demand products that make their daily lives easier, more satisfying, or both. Even five decades later, millions of Americans have decided that is precisely what hippie products and consumer ideas do for them. As you will see, the hippie philosophy and aesthetic are behind so much of what we take for granted in our daily lives, helping to bring into popular culture everything from organic food and faded jeans and yoga classes and jewelry for men, to the long-lasting *Lord of the Rings* and *Siddhartha* crazes, to Snapple and Celestial Seasoning herbal tea drinks, and even to the underpinnings of the personal computer and the Internet.

The Haight-Ashbury hippie movement was an all-out assault on the mainstream culture that propelled a shifting of many traditional American values to the hippie point of view. So today non-hippies across the political spectrum, who would never think to associate their lives with the counter-culture of the sixties, have had their tastes in food, fashion, music, religion, recreation, and lifestyle altered by the original hippies, their disciples and adopters. In business terms this adds up to a bonanza. If all of the products created or popularized by the hippies were part of one corporation —Hippie, inc.— it would be *one of the most successful businesses in the world*.

WHAT IS A HIPPIE?

In the most general sense, a hippie is someone who, upon entering young adulthood, rejects the core values of his or her family, community, and society and who seeks to replace those values with markedly different ones, truer to his or her emerging adult self. Tensions between teenagers and their parents are not uncommon, but hippies should not to be confused with garden-variety teenage rebels. Although adolescents acting out can pose real concerns, with drinking and drugs, crashed cars, and unwanted pregnancies, their estrangement from their childhood community is usually short-lived. Rebellious youths tend to return to their communities after a period of hell-raising, to live out their days espousing the same values and beliefs they earlier opposed. In contrast, true hippies rarely go home again, either literally or figuratively, and seldom revert to the values they grew up with.

Each generation offers us their own version of hippies, who disrupt the social fabric with new ideas and ideals that challenge the mainstream and provoke and stimulate change. However, the small band of original hippies who lived in or near the Haight-Ashbury district of San Francisco between the Fall of 1965 and the Fall of 1967, along with their hippie acid-testing cohorts in Santa Cruz, has had an impact on our society unlike that of any other subculture before or since. From the beginning of the movement, stories about the hippies were heavily skewed toward the strange characters and bizarre tales that sell magazines and boost TV ratings. But the media made a critical omission when reporters failed to distinguish between the hundreds of sincere original hippies and the thousands of uncommitted hippie poseurs and runaway youth that piled into San Francisco shortly after the movement began.

WHO WERE THE ORIGINAL HIPPIES?

The original hippies lived and worked primarily in a 28-square-block area in San Francisco. In the first few months of 1966, not counting runaways, they numbered approximately 800. They were ordinary men and women questioning the world they had inherited from their parents. Some were Eagle scouts, others Korean War veterans and Holocaust survivors. There was a jewel thief, a jug band player, a greeting card artist, a grandniece of Leon Trotsky, an Olympic-level wrestler, and a descendent of Andrew Jackson. Many of them never liked the word hippie and some, even today, disassociate themselves from that label, which was imposed on the Haight-Ashbury community by the media. Within the counter-culture community there were different groups. The Diggers—a guerrilla street theater group—didn't think of themselves as hippies. Nor did Ken Kesey, who said he was "too young to have been a beat and too old to have been a hippie," however, popular history disagrees, and he is remembered as a principle trendsetter of the sixties' counterculture and one of the first hippies. Other members of the Haight-Ashbury community who accept that they were part of the original hippies, differentiate themselves from the thousands of hippies who came later: the vicarious hippies, the plastic hippies. The musicians, artists, Diggers, Pranksters, merchants, druggies and assorted other non-mainstream groups did not always share the same philosophy or exhibit the same behavior. However, as flawed as the label hippies is, it does contain fifty years of collective memory. So for the purpose of this book, rather than coin a new label, we will continue the historical use of the term hippies to define the Haight-Ashbury counter-culture community of the sixties, an amazing group of people regardless of what you call them.

The stereotype of the "hippie slacker" does not hold true for the original hippies, especially when applied to the hippie leaders mentioned in this book. They were outstandingly productive—intellectually, artistically, and in the business world. A surprisingly large proportion of these leaders were former U.S. military personnel, including some who earned high distinctions in combat. Many were former students of some of the most prestigious institutions of higher learning in the U.S. None of the leaders mentioned in this book were baby boomers (i.e., all were born before 1946) and none were members of the Communist Party. One stereotype that is true and ultimately worked to their and the country's advantage stands to this day: they were non-conformist to the core. Their willingness—even eagerness—to go against the grain turned off some Americans; nonetheless, it was precisely this quality that led to so many successful innovations.

The original hippies embraced an ethos that included the principles of equality, self-knowledge, and universal oneness. They believed that all people and things are connected to each other, no one is better or worse, all have inherent value, and all achieve their highest potential when they commit to doing the act or conducting the life that is true to themselves. The

earliest hippies asserted that the successful pursuit of human fulfillment is accomplished through a process of self-awareness facilitated by the use of certain drugs, the instructions of religious writings and teachers, and the practice of intrapersonal and interpersonal transparency. This ethos shares some commonality with the ethos of the Transcendentalists of the nineteenth century. Whether it be Ralph Waldo Emerson's emphasis on self-reliance or Henry David Thoreau's connecting with the natural world, the hippies shared characteristics with this and other historic subcultures who railed against the establishment and believed in bettering themselves and creating a better world.

PRODUCTS AND IDEAS

Though this book focuses on its consumer accomplishments, fundamentally the Haight-Ashbury hippie movement was not a consumer movement built on economic principles, but a social movement based on philosophical beliefs that undergirded the hippie leaders' push for social change. In interviews that I conducted between 2009 and 2015 with some of the original hippie business men and women the phrase "it was the right thing to do" was a common refrain. They also talked of a moral code guiding their business decisions whether it be investing in an underground newspaper like *The San Francisco Oracle* or setting up a network to distribute free food like the Diggers' Free Store.

Grounded by the belief that they were conducting their lives and businesses in a civically and morally responsible way, in a one-hundred week period that began on the evening of November 27, 1965, at Ken Kesey's and the Merry Pranksters' first public acid test and ended on the afternoon of October 6, 1967, at the Diggers funeral march, this small original hippie community conceived or popularized innovative ideas and products that, over the course of the next five decades, created employment for millions of Americans, pumped billions of dollars into the nation's economy, transformed U.S. consumer culture and business practices, and shaped *the most commercially lucrative social movement in American history.*

This provocative assertion runs contrary to most descriptions of hippies in the media. This book looks at the hippies through the lens of business. It attempts, through both fact-based and circumstantial evidence to corroborate the argument that hippie products and ideas led to enormous wealth creation by hippies, hippie disciples, and non-hippie adopters. While in rare cases the products or ideas that I credit to the hippies were original, more often than not they were either a reshaping or popularizing of existing products and ideas. The hippies acted as prescient advocates and popularizers of products that eventually became widely successful. They were also geniuses at "continuous innovation"—taking an existing product or idea and tweaking it, adding a flavor and making it their own. Most of the hippie innovations were not "radical innovations" like the airplane which have an immediate, obvious, and profound effect on the culture. "Continuous innovation" is subtler and slower and not always as clearly identified with an inventor. An innovation may be as simple as taking a product like jeans, which have been around for hundreds of years, and intentionally damaging them with holes and tears.

From natural and organic food stores to screen-printed t-shirts to marijuana to light shows to the folk/rock music industry, hippies were either originators or popularizers of these products. There were also many commercially-viable ideas that were bandied about in the hey-day of the hippie movement, including recycling, alternative energy, non-competitive leisure (like Frisbees), the shop local/buy local movement, a "freetail" pricing policy, sexualized advertising styles, flat management structures, and "less is more." Quite often the hippies were promulgating these ideas and products when most Americans were moving in the opposite direction.

FIFTY YEAR PERSPECTIVE

This book tells the economic story of the original hippies. It is a story that runs directly counter to the notion that the hippie movement was a passing fad with few enduring achievements and even fewer business successes. Hippies tend to be remembered either through a haze of romantic nostalgia, as long-haired, barefoot flower children advocating peace and love, or through a lens of disapproval, as filthy, foul-mouthed, promiscuous trouble-makers and drug addicts. Neither vision is entirely wrong, but neither recognizes the ongoing constructive legacy the original hippies left us.

In recent years there have been several books published that highlight the alternative view of the hippies as an influential counterculture voice re-shaping the world, from the personal computer (*What The Dormouse Said: How the Sixties Counter-Culture Shaped the Personal Computer Industry* by John Markoff, a Pulitzer prize-winning author and New York Times technology reporter), to the Internet (*From Counterculture to Cyberculture: Stewart Brand, the Whole Earth Network, and the Rise of Digital Utopianism* by Fred Turner, an Associate Professor in the Department of Communication at Stanford University and Director of Stanford's Program in Science, Technology, and Society) to fashion (*Hippie Chic* by Lauren D. Whitley, curator in the department of Textile and Fashion Arts at the Museum of Fine Arts, Boston) to physics (*How the Hippies Saved Physics* by David Kaiser, the Germeshausen Professor of the History of Science at the Massachusetts Institute of Technology [MIT], and head of its Science, Technology, and Society program). What these four books have in common, besides highly accomplished authors, is communicating the extensive influence of the hippies and the counter-culture of the sixties on the mainstream culture. According to these authors, the hippies, their ideas, their products, and their values helped shape the clothes we wear, the computers we use, our understanding of quantum mechanics, and the making of the modern Internet world, supporting the assertion that the hippies' reach extends well beyond LSD and love beads.

This book focuses on the original hippies and their accomplishments during the first 100 weeks of the movement. Their achievements after the demise of Haight-Ashbury are also briefly addressed, as well as the contributions of hippie disciples, because part of the original hippies' legacy is the world that was created based on their beliefs and practices.

My journey into this subculture has led me to conclude several things:

First, the view that the original hippie movement basically came to nothing—or worse that it contributed to the unraveling of the country's moral fiber—is simplistic and overstated.

Disgruntled Resident

Second, that their passionate, innovative spirit—a blend of entrepreneurship, proselytizing, and mischief has helped to shape the country's consumer culture over the last fifty years.

Third, that it was precisely their bizarre and unconventional, yet remarkably rational, even sober approach to daily life and consumption (attributes they had in common with later idea innovators like Bill Gates and Michael Dell, and business thinkers like Stephen Covey) that led some original Haight-Ashbury hippies to create and others to passionately advocate dozens of new product innovations, commercial practices and business philosophies that mainstream America embraces today. Many of the beliefs and

Early on: Mod and Beat Styles Coexist

totems of the hippie movement are now part of our everyday lives and much of our current value system—the way we eat, dress, recreate, worship, consume, and relate to the world around us—is a byproduct of that movement. This counter-culture movement may be measured not only by the enduring changes it brought about to the culture but also its influence on the creation of new American wealth. I conservatively estimate that the business ideas and ventures begun or popularized by the original hippies to be worth by 2016 hundreds of billions of dollars.

How did they do it?

PART I

*

ORIGINS

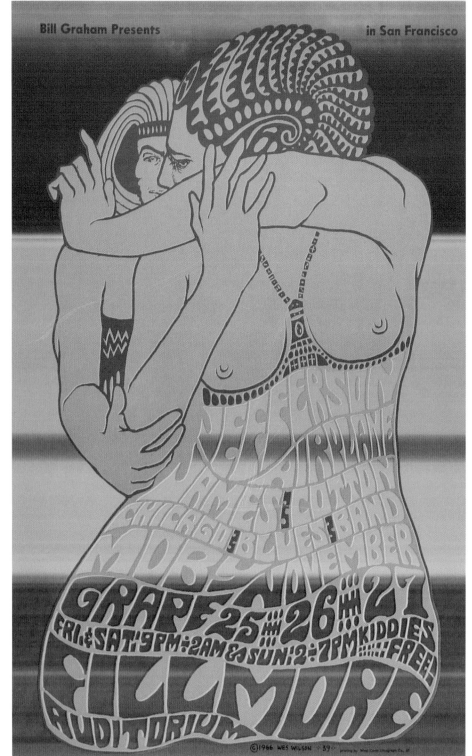

1

PREHISTORY OF
THE HIPPIES

*Many of the hippies began as beats; they came out of North Beach
and spread like a rainbow into Haight-Ashbury.*

—Julius Karpen

THREE SIGNIFICANT YOUTH movements took place in California in the 1950s, 1960s, and 1970s. The original Haight-Ashbury hippies were distinct from the Beats who emerged in the North Beach neighborhood in the fifties, and from the campus activists who got their start with the Berkeley Free Speech Movement in 1964 and burgeoned across the country during the civil rights struggles and anti-war protests of the late sixties and early seventies. The three movements ran more or less consecutively, spanning nearly two decades, and much of their incipient activities took place within a twenty-mile radius. Indeed, the fit and adventurous can easily visit, by bicycle in a single day, the centers of three of the most radical youth movements in U.S. history.

BEATS

(The beats) were . . . uptight as hell.

—Toni Del Renzio, **The Flower Children**

The hippies were indebted to the beatniks, or beats, who paved the way for a discontented subculture in post-World War II America. The beats saw the mainstream culture as deadening. They were anti-materialistic and were looking to create a more spiritual community. In San Francisco the beats lived in North Beach, which had a history as a haven for outcasts. A magnet for gold seekers beginning in 1849, North Beach business boomed, attracting many customers and owners with dubious pasts—men like Australian Francis Christie (a.k.a. Frank Gardiner) who bought the Twilight Star Saloon on Kearney Street in the North Beach neighborhood in 1874, twelve years after masterminding the largest gold robbery in Australian history (his take is valued today at approximately 12.5 million). North Beach and adjacent Barbary Coast were described by Benjamin Lloyd in 1876 as teeming with outlaws and prostitutes and bursting at the seams with "licentiousness, debauchery, pollutions, loathsome disease, insanity . . . misery, poverty, wealth, profanity, blasphemy . . . death . . . and hell."

By the 1950s, North Beach was the home to Beat cellar clubs, live poetry readings, and impromptu jazz sessions. The North Beach scene attracted performers that included Maya Angelou, Bill Cosby, Tom and Dick Smothers, Phyllis Diller, Miles Davis, and John Coltrane.

At first glance, it looked as if it were the beats, not the hippies, who were destined to become a cultural and financial success. City Lights Books, (located at 262 Columbus Street) started in 1953 by well-known writer Lawrence Ferlinghetti, is still a fabulous store today, attracting tourists from all over the world.

Caffe Trieste (601 Vallejo Street) was begun in 1956 by the Giotta family who had just immigrated to America from Italy (Francis Ford Coppola supposedly wrote his script for *The Godfather* at one of its tables). The café, which continues to this day, claims to be the first coffee shop in America to sell espresso.

The Purple Onion (140 Columbus Street) was a beat cellar club that opened in 1952. Comedians like Woody Allen, Phyllis Diller, and Lenny Bruce played there. Maya Angelou performed there and so did the Kingston Trio. The Smothers Brothers, who later went on to have their own hit TV show, began their career there.

Jazz and poetry readings started in North Beach at The Cellar (567 Green Street) in 1956 when Poet Ruth Weiss began reading poetry one evening in the middle of a jazz set, creating a new form of entertainment. The art form spread to other clubs and Allen Ginsberg and Jack Kerouac read at The Place (1546 Grant Street), a well-known Beat establishment.

The Jazz Workshop (471 Broadway) was home to many jazz greats, including Art Blakey, Ornette Coleman, John Coltrane, Miles Davis, and Sonny Rollins. Before Janis Joplin went on to become a hippie blues/rock singer, she was doing gigs at the Workshop for $10 a night. (John Helms, brother of the legendary concert promoter Chet Helms, relates how Janis got to San Francisco in the first place:)

> So, about in early 1963, I was still at home, about 19, and there was knock at the door one evening and it was Chet and Janis. They had hitchhiked to Fort Worth from Austin, Texas. I didn't know who Janis was at the time. I remember that Chet was standing in the front of the door and that his appearance had changed and he looked like an English Lord with his Beatle-like length of hair. And there was this girl behind him who was quietly strumming an autoharp and singing, and I remember that she had a natural hair-do that wasn't typical in that day. Through the screen door, Chet asked my mother if it was okay if he and Janis spent the night together, and my mother said no because she was very religious. She was a Fundamentalist Christian and the daughter of a Baptist preacher but also very loving to us all. She said they were welcome to have dinner with us. After dinner, Chet and Janis asked if I would drive them to the highway so they could head out to the West Coast. They were hoping to get Janis a gig in the North Beach clubs. So after dinner, Janis and Chet and I drove out to the highway in my '55 Ford. I left them on the side of the road with their thumbs out. I guess you could say that the rest is history.

Janis Joplin and Chet Helms are representative of a group of beats who evolved into the Neo-Beats just prior to the hippie movement. A small group of shaggy-headed thinkers, the Neo-Beats were itching to break out of a society they saw as growing increasingly "plastic." While the rest of the nation

Janis Joplin and Chet Helms before they became famous

watched Lucy and Desi, this group of "bohemian tweeners"—Neo-Beats—worked and played quietly between 1960 and 1965, reading Alan Watts and Rachel Carson, gradually transforming from beats who took themselves too seriously to hippies who couldn't keep their fingers off the play button.

The first Neo-Beat hangout opened in 1960 when Bob Stubbs, a North Beach beat who had recently relocated to the Haight opened a coffee shop, The Blue Unicorn, located near the corner of Ashbury and Hayes Street. As rent prices in North Beach started rising, the migration to the Haight began in earnest. The Unicorn became a gathering place for beats fleeing pricey North Beach. At least ten men, all customers of the Unicorn, assumed the look of a hippie, growing out their hair and beards several years before the hippie movement began.

Writer Burton Wolfe first mentioned the names of these ten individuals in his 1968 book, *The Hippies*. Of course, he couldn't have known then just what these ten would eventually accomplish.

* Allen Cohen
* Paul Krassner
* Michael Bowen
* Allen Ginsberg
* Michael McClure
* Tsvi Strauch
* Charles Artman
* Tosh
* Dick Edverett
* Wallace Healy

Two of the ten men listed above would go on to found their own newspapers (Cohen and Krassner); one would eventually have his art displayed in the Whitney Museum (Bowen); two would become internationally-recognized writers (Ginsberg and McClure); and one (Strauch) would pioneer the "hippie retail" business in the Haight.

This group of bohemians, Neo-Beat women and men became some of the most influential hippies in the Haight-Ashbury movement and several played critical roles in the creation of *Hippie, inc.*

RADICALS—1950–1965

During the late fifties there were only a few radicals at Berkeley. They belonged to groups like the Young Communists, the Young Socialists, and a left-wing Zionist group. I estimate that there were no more than 40 of us bearded guys out of 10,000 students at Berkeley. Political radicalism was something the European students did, not the Americans. We had just come out of WWII and the country was making a lot of money. We didn't want to stop that. We had a General for a President (Dwight D. Eisenhower)—and when he spoke, we all saluted and followed orders. *Life* magazine named us "the silent generation," and they were right. The guys all dressed like The Kingston Trio—red sweaters, ironed buttoned-down shirts, hair neatly cut, toothy smiles. Funny enough—the manager of The Kingston Trio, Frank Werber, according to his obituary, was arrested by federal agents and accused of conspiracy to transport hundreds of pounds of Mexican pot. So there was this other world going on, you see, that few Americans knew anything about. And it was getting ready to explode.

—*Tsvi Strauch*

In the late 1950s, Professor Kenneth Kenniston, a Yale adolescent psychologist and one of the most respected developmental psychologists in the world at the time, was commissioned to write a series of articles on American youth that commenced toward the end of the beat movement and stopped several years after the end of the hippie movement.

He wrote:

In 1960: "Overt rebellion (on the part of American youth) is extremely rare."

Allen Ginsberg at the Human Be-In, January 1966

In 1962: "For many young people, it is essential to stay 'cool,' and 'coolness' involves detachment, lack of commitment, never being enthusiastic."

In 1963: "Our men and women remain overwhelmingly uninterested in the state of the nation and the world. *The apolitical stance* of American youth is something of a puzzle."

This period (1960–1963), which Kenniston characterized as one of detached coolness and non-involvement on the part of American youth, and others consider to be "dead years"—a time in which America's youth was surprisingly reticent and uncommitted to any cause save their own betterment—coincided with the years John Kennedy was president of the United States. Long-haired, barefooted youth were yet to arrive *en masse*, and, in the early 1960s, outright youth rebellion was all but unheard of in North Beach, the Haight-Ashbury district, or anywhere else in the country except for a few isolated protesters and a small group of black and white Freedom Riders.

Still, the detached apathetic political attitude Kenniston described as present in the first few years of the decade was only *partially* correct. *Most* American youth from 1960–1965 wanted little more than a new car, a secure job, and a home in the suburbs—but not all. There were, in fact, pockets of dissent.

Hundreds of America's young people were becoming engaged in politics and social reform between 1960 and 1963 due to President Kennedy's and Sargent Shriver's creation of the Peace Corps which, along with the Civil Rights marches organized by Dr. Martin Luther King, Jr., and others in the southern U.S., allowed America's youth who were so inclined to develop and express their political and social conscience. In places far from San Francisco—cities as distinctly different as Birmingham, Alabama and Ann Arbor, Michigan—the steam of youthful dissent was quietly and constructively released by personal acts of social reform and economic and educational development in the years leading up to the hippie movement. Underlying the student's activism was a sincere trust in their leaders, particularly, President Kennedy, his brother, Robert, and Martin Luther King, Jr., a fact that helps us understand why things changed so abruptly when the President was killed.

Technically speaking, both the Civil Rights Movement and the Peace Corps initiative were not *youth* movements. That's because both were largely conceived of and led by *adults* (namely, King and the Kennedy brothers)—30- and 40-something-year-old leaders who, while extremely successful at winning the respect of 20-something Americans as well as rallying and recruiting them for a good cause, were themselves still part of established adult institutions—the church and the government.

Other adult-led institutions were the universities such as the University of Michigan (home to Tom Hayden and other S.D.S.—Students for a Democratic Society—members who were instrumental in drafting the Port Huron

Statement in 1962, outlining a New Left vision of the future), and the University of California, Berkeley, where in 1964 Mario Savio became one of the leaders of the Free Speech movement, organizing protests and demanding the University lift its ban on political activities on campus. This was soon followed by civil rights and anti-war protests on campus and confrontations with the police. These protests soon spread to other colleges throughout the United States.

HIPPIES

The hippies said, *"Fuck that!* Fuck the way it has always been done. We're doing it the way it should be done." And that is the attitude of every great American innovator and every successful entrepreneur, from Thomas Edison to Sam Walton. They're audacious, they're pushy, and more often than not, they're right."

—*Lou Honary*

Across the bay from Berkeley, there was another group of disaffected youth, mainly in their mid-to-late twenties, who felt a sense of *wrongness* when they arrived in the Haight in the early to mid-sixties. This wrongness encompassed not just the nation's political and social ills and the perils of a nuclear arms race but also what businesses were perpetrating upon the American people. They saw technological advances and increasing mechanization as profoundly alienating. They perceived the American consumer as estranged. They saw it as wrong to deceptively promote products that were sickening and sometimes even killing their purchasers, and wrong to engage in enterprises that impoverished the country's economic bulwark: family farms, locally owned businesses, and day laborers. And so, in the words of several hippie leaders they decided, "Fuck it!" Not an anarchist, destruction-for-its-own-sake kind of fuck-it and not a cynical Beat-style fuck-it, but fuck-it in the sense of: "Let's admit that certain products and ways of doing business are morally reprehensible, and let's start anew. Let's find a better way."

For most of them this meant a holistic, *carpe diem* approach to life. If all might soon be lost in a nuclear holocaust, they could at least enjoy their lives in the meantime. They embraced the comforts of home using natural materials, ate locally grown vegetables, home-made yogurt, and whole grains, drank warm herbal teas, and wore soft cotton and wool. They enjoyed mind-expanding drugs and ecstatic music and dance, in a kind of metaphorical reaction to the Cold War and to a society that seemed to be getting harsher and "colder" every day.

This group of mostly young adults worried about their country, regarded Jesus Christ and Buddha as their heroes, generally displayed respect for law enforcement even when it wasn't reciprocated, and were regularly involved in the social problems of their neighborhood. They established formal systems of distributing food and clothing to those in need, set up their own medical clinic, and opened new clothing boutiques, food stores, cafes, and other retail establishments. A seemingly disproportionate number were unusually intelligent and ambitious: graduates of Harvard, Berkeley, Columbia, Grinnell, and Yale; scientists, PhDs and MDs, former corporate executives, classically trained musicians, distinguished servicemen, best-selling authors, self-made millionaires, and certified geniuses. A high percentage of them embraced a long-standing American entrepreneurial spirit. These earliest hippies set out not to overthrow the system, but to rectify it, by creating a new economy that would be true to their values. Values which, in hindsight, appear to be foundational to their achievements.

The hippie values—love, peace, acceptance of all, transparency, individual freedom to fulfill one's potential, all are one, all are equal—were initially scoffed at as impractical pipe dreams that bore no relation to successful commerce. Persisting, these principles served as markers for success that guided hippie business strategy framed by the goal of making products that were safe and useful, that preserved the planet in their consumption, and that ultimately served the good of all, not just a few. Organic supermarkets, tie-dye t-shirts, and interactive, online communities are just three of many innovations that grew out of a values-based approach that served as the common thread and creative blueprint of hippie inventiveness.

However, there is no one-size-fits-all way to describe a hippie business man or woman. They were by definition nonconformists, and they certainly didn't all think alike. Consider the two Thelin brothers, owners of the Haight's Psychedelic Shop, who were very influential in the original hippie movement. Jay Thelin was much more business minded in his approach and even contemplated franchising the Psychedelic Shop but Ron was opposed to this idea so they let it die. Ron was influenced by the Diggers (who declared the death of money.) Many of the Diggers came out of the San Francisco Mime Troupe, and they were more political activists in their approach to problems on the street.

> Ron and I got along really well together. He was a much better athlete than I was and I was a little better as a scholar. I handled the business end of the shop and he engaged in the political and social endeavors that made the Haight the hippest place to be in America. He was not necessarily anti-business but rather anti-exploitation, anti-greed and anti-military industrial complex. We were team players with different ideas on how to reach our goals—that's all.
>
> —*Jay Thelin*

The Thelin brothers held a special status among the original hippies, who regarded them as the quintessential hippies, the major hippies. Hometown boys, Ron and Jay's father managed the Woolworth store on Haight street in the early 1940's when they were toddlers. The family moved to San Mateo and when the boys were midway through elementary school they moved again to San Luis Obispo. After serving in the army, these former Eagle Scouts were drawn to the growing counter-culture movement in San Francisco. Part of their mystique comes from the fact that they opened what is believed to be the first head shop in the United States, The Psychedelic Shop at 1535 Haight Street, on January 3, 1966, right across the street from their father's old store. It became *the* place for hippies to buy their rolling papers, bongs, underground newspapers and adult comics—the hippie retail epicenter.

Although Ron may not have had an entrepreneur's heart (the store lasted less than two years) both brothers had the inspiration to open a new kind of store; decades later, head shops and shops devoted to hippie paraphernalia still dot the retail landscape. However, their more measurable contribution to Hippie, inc., has to do with a substance *not* legally sold across their counter. Though, according to Jay they never sold drugs, their store promoted LSD and marijuana with the distribution of psychedelic art, literature and information about psychedelic chemicals like LSD which was still legal in California until October, 1966.

For many, at the time, drugs provided more than a simple high. Pot and LSD sales were a major source of business financing. As Tsvi Strauch said, "Look, almost everyone dealt dope in those days. For a lot of businesspeople, it was kind of like having a money tree in the backyard. Need a little extra money to pay this month's rent? Just deal a little pot or acid and voilà—the rent is paid!"

The hippies weren't the only ones promoting, growing and selling marijuana, but they became the main disseminators of the daily practice and joys of pot and some of the biggest dealers. And their disciples were the majority of the population who branched out across California and other states to start the clandestine farms which have grown into sizable illegal and legal businesses. In 2010 marijuana was one of the top-3 largest agricultural products in the country. Harvard University's Jeffrey Miron estimated the size of the marijuana market to be between $17 and 20 billion annually (compared to corn at $20 billion and soy beans at $17 billion).

The movement to legalize marijuana also had its roots in hippie culture. In the book *Hippies: A Guide to an American Subculture*, Micah L. Issitt, writes,

> As a whole, the hippies believed that the government should not have the right to impose laws on consensual activities. The standard argument was that the government had no right to tell people what to do with their bodies, whether it was taking drugs or having sex. . . .While the hippies were not the first subculture to resist the curtailment of consensual crime, they brought the issue to the forefront of society. . . . One natural outgrowth of this "revolutionary" opposition was the movement to legalize marijuana.

The very first public organization to advocate for the legalization of marijuana originated in Haight-Ashbury. A little-known organization, LEMAR

Jay and Ron Thelin

Summer of Love

("legalize marijuana") took up the cause in 1966 when few were ready to embrace it and HALO—Haight-Ashbury Legal Organization—provided some of the first lawyers to represent clients busted for marijuana.

BEATS VS HIPPIES

> To me, the beats were intellectual and very thoughtful people who were interested in 'the greater good.' The hippies were pleasure seekers —you know, Dionysian. It's like the beats were the parents and the hippies were the unruly kids.
>
> —*Mark Braunstein*

The beats had successful businesses, they had a head start, famous names, and a best selling book, *On The Road,* by Jack Kerouac. The beats, however, never went viral, and the hippies did. Why was it the hippies and not the beats who had such a profound effect on U.S. consumer culture?

One answer is that the beats never gained traction partly because the impact of the beat movement was limited geographically to coastal America (specifically, San Francisco and New York City) and time-wise, from 1953 to 1963. So most Americans had no firsthand encounter with beats, drawing their conclusion from sparse media reports and Hollywood caricatures. Another answer was simply that the beats, with few exceptions, were too dark, too beaten down. The hippies were lighter, more fun-oriented.

Comparing the two groups, character-wise, the beats were:

* dark

* anxious

* politically and socially disconnected

* detached and critical "spectators"

* intellectuals and pseudo-intellectuals

Whereas the hippies were:

* playful
* enthusiastic
* relaxed
* politically and socially active
* open to new product and ideas
* engaged and hopeful "players"

The products and businesses of the two groups followed suit. Beat products included:

* absurd theater
* caffeine stimulants, usually in the form of heavy Italian coffee
* unfiltered cigarettes
* complex jazz scores
* inscrutable poetry
* hard liquor

Whereas hippie products included:

* jewelry and beads

Sue Swanson (wearing glasses), with Phil Lesh and Bob Weir (standing behind her)

* psychedelic posters
* aromatic joss sticks
* colorful clothing and accessories
* drugs that relaxed, such as pot and LSD
* loud, easy-to-understand, electrified music, albums, and concerts.

Like comparing a '59 Edsel to a '66 Corvette, the beats were a depressingly hard sell, the hippies, a marketer's dreams come true. The hippies were optimistic, hopeful, sexualized, outspoken, experiential, experimental, intensely personal, change-makers, opinionated, risk-takers, attuned to the importance of symbols, and innovative. In other words, they were the future.

RADICALS VS HIPPIES

Though there was intense polarization between the young and the old during the sixties, and a synergy that existed among the hippies and radicals —both cultures rebelling against the establishment—the two groups did not always share common goals or values, and at times clashed. Many Berkeley radicals looked down on the hippies for their refusal to participate in their political rallies and their emphasis on the spiritual. Tsvi Strauch bluntly states:

> The Berkeley crowd would complain because we wouldn't come to their fucking marches. You know, we tried to build a relationship with the Berkeley leaders and eventually we started to work together. I know it sounds self-serving, but the Berkeley group was in awe of the hippies. Problem was, we weren't in awe of them—we felt there were other ways to get the word out than marching on Washington and raising hell. You can see this in retrospect, right? The campus radicals began to look like us—growing beards and hair. In contrast, we never started to look like them in their thin black ties and Ivy League jackets.

The hippies recoiled from the "bad vibes" they felt emanating from the angry radicals and, in the can-do fashion of hippies, they tried an unorthodox solution:

> The Haight-Ashbury scene was dedicated to Turn On, Tune In, Drop Out. The Berkeley scene was still locked into an activist mode that came out of the Free Speech Movement. We both wanted to achieve the same things regarding the war in Vietnam and racial equality but our approach was a bit different. What happened was several of us in the Haight met with several of the Berkeley folks and proposed they try some pot and have a look at our approach. This meeting went well

Ben Van Meter (center), with Jerry Slick (right)

and it seemed to us, at the time, that getting turned on had a profound effect on the Berkeley scene. The radical efforts did not abate and, of course, the Democratic convention of 1968 was based on confrontation and direct action. The hippie contribution might have been the flowers in the gun barrels.

—*Jay Thelin*

Another fundamental difference between the campus radicals and the original hippies has to do with when they were born and the state of the U.S.

economy at that time. Most of the early Haight-Ashbury hippies—including the business leaders in Hippie, inc.—were born between 1934 and 1944, between the Great Depression and the close of the Second World War. In contrast, the baby boomers, who made up the bulk of the late-1960s campus radicals, were born after World War II during one of the greatest economic expansions in U.S. history. Hence, most of the campus activists had affluent, or at least comfortable, childhoods, whereas the original hippies only began to benefit from the incredible strength of the U.S. economy at about the time they left home to start college or begin their careers.

Many hippies experienced not just the vestiges of Depression-era poverty but also the stresses of World War II. (Two of the hippie entrepreneurs profiled in this book, Frank Werber and Tsvi Strauch, were born in Vienna and escaped Nazi-controlled Austria. A third, Bill Graham, was a Berlin-born Jewish child first sent to France and then smuggled to America after France fell to the Nazis. He lost most of his family in the Holocaust, and reinvented himself in New York City before moving to San Francisco.) A significant proportion of the original hippies served in the military during the Korean War, where they developed a type of discipline and dedication that perhaps only wartime service can teach. During their teenage and young adult years the Cold War was at its height, and the threat of nuclear annihilation had a real and profound effect on their world view. These challenging economic and social forces created in the original hippies a sense of urgency as well as a longing for societal change. The original hippies were only a few years older than the campus radicals but a few years sometimes is a different era, especially when they contain the remnants of a nationwide Depression and a World War.

GENERATION GAP

As different as the hippies and radicals were, they were united in their rejection of the establishment. Why was it that both groups, promising and ambitious young people, becoming adults just as their nation achieved unprecedented power and wealth, instead of joining the mainstream and cashing in, turned away from their elders and rejected their values, creating what the media loves to call the "generation gap?"

The shift from the adult-led Civil Rights marches to youth-led demonstrations and rebellion in Berkeley and the Haight didn't *have* to happen. Indeed, older adults might have exerted their leadership over the young—just as they had for decades prior—well beyond 1963. *So why didn't they?* Simply, the shift in leadership from adults to youth resulted from a loss of trust. Whereas American youth in the early sixties were willing to be led by adults who, at the time they *implicitly* trusted, this attitude of trust began to dry up shortly after Kennedy's assassination and by the time of the hippies, it had completely evaporated. Adding to the mistrust were conspiracy theories that roped high-ranking officials (including Lyndon Johnson) into the ring of suspects involved in the assassination of the President and ongoing exposure of CIA hijinks in foreign countries where its nefarious activities included the assassination and the overthrow of democratically-elected leaders and governments. Another explanation for this erosion of trust was offered by original hippie, Robert Limon:

> Take smoking, for example. The adults were telling us that cigarettes don't hurt you—they even had medical doctors saying this. But we knew better. We saw our parents and other adults getting sick with this stuff and dying of lung cancer. So, we saw right through it—it was all a lie. That's one of the reasons cigarettes were not popular with the hippies—they were seen as "the man, yet again, trying to pull the wool over our eyes." The adults in our lives were, in essence, willing to lie to us and even put our lives at risk just to make a buck. It was that kind of deception and moral compromise that made us feel like no adult could be trusted to tell the truth. How could we trust the adults' decision about Vietnam? We were the ones getting killed, not them. We'd either have to take the lead or watch the country go to hell in a handbasket.

Dubbed "The Greatest Generation" by journalist Tom Brokaw and others, parents of the hippies and campus radicals were seemingly better at winning

Monica Collier and Allen Cohen (in front of the Psychedelic Shop)

wars than at winning their children's trust. Consequently, the lid on overt and extreme political activism and dissent among the youth slowly and precariously began to lift.

Allen Cohen, one of the founders of *The San Francisco Oracle*—underground hippie newspaper—defined the dual assault from the radicals and the hippies on the establishment:

> The political rebellion was forged in the Civil Rights struggle, the S.D.S. Port Huron Statement, the Free Speech Movement in Berkeley and the beginning of the anti-war movement. The rebellion was radical with an extreme democratic openness, mistrustful and independent of political parties or dogmas, anti-authority and non-hierarchical, generally non-violent, and dedicated to the values of equality, justice and peace.
>
> The cultural rebellion was birthed by the Beat literary explosion, the Leary LSD experiments at Harvard, rock and roll music, the Haight-Ashbury Renaissance and the Human Be-In. It was anti-materialist, idealistic, anarchistic, surreal, Dionysian and transcendental. This two headed rebellion was now the greatest threat to the American status quo since the Depression.

A non-hippie voice, Professor Kenniston, continuing his survey after the Free Speech and Vietnam War campus protests and hippie movement had begun, wrote

In 1966: Only now do we find any significant number of students prepared to criticize society.

In 1967: The apparent upsurge of dissent among American college students is one of the most puzzling phenomena in American society.

In 1971: No issue today divides as does youthful opposition.

2

THE BIG BANG
—DAY ONE

ORIGINAL HIPPIE: KEN KESEY

BURTON WOLFE SAYS in *The Hippies,* that Kesey "was the prankster who did more than any other to create the hippie movement." In small, intimate settings where people took LSD, listened to music and danced, his Acid Tests served as early incarnations of the drug-fueled rock concerts and other mass gatherings that followed, events typically associated with the hippies. His parties, networking, speeches, merry prankster bus rides, antics and physical presence were all influential. So was his most popular book, *One Flew Over The Cuckoo's Nest,* whose main character, Randle McMurphy, is a charming rebel locked up in a mental hospital, who questions authority in words and actions.

A renaissance man of extraordinary gifts—best-selling author, Olympic caliber wrestler, and charismatic leader—Kesey would have been a stand-out in whatever generation he came to manhood. In a 2010 interview, Penelope DeVries, an original hippie, said of Kesey: "My impression of Ken was that he was going to do something big, whether or not he had money. Of course, he made a lot of money from the sale of his books, but money-making wasn't his main thing and he would have been successful regardless of how many books he wrote and sold."

Growing up on a dairy farm in Oregon, Kesey had an imposing build which he put to good use, hunting and fishing and playing football and wrestling in high school. As a teenager he became fascinated by the theater, ventriloquism, hypnotism, and all forms of magic. He won an award for best thespian in high school and his classmates voted him most likely to succeed.

He attended the University of Oregon on a wrestling scholarship and was chosen as an alternate for the 1960 Olympic wrestling team. In the classroom he majored in theater arts and writing. Neither his artist friends nor his fellow athletes understood his associating with the other.

Initially he aspired to be an actor and spent college summers trying to land bit parts in Los Angeles. But by the time he graduated in 1957—the year Jack Kerouac's *On the Road* was published—Kesey had focused his creative energies on becoming a writer. He began a never-published novel about college athletes titled *End of Autumn*. The next year he won a Woodrow Wilson Fellowship to Stanford University.

The following two years of Kesey's education changed the course of his life and helped spawn the hippie movement. In school Kesey honed his craft under the tutelage of novelist Wallace Stegner and famed editor Malcolm Cowley and found creative inspiration in an exceptional group of classmates, which included Robert Stone, Larry McMurtry, Wendell Berry, and the man who would become his life-long friend and partner in mischief, Ken Babbs. A different kind of education took place off campus. Kesey lived in a bohemian neighborhood in Menlo Park with his wife and childhood sweetheart Faye Haxby. There he hobnobbed with Neal Cassady and Allen Ginsberg and was introduced to the pleasures of wine and marijuana, the work of Kerouac, William Burroughs, Lawrence Ferlinghetti, and other cutting-edge writers, and the outside-the-box thinking of the nearby North Beach Beat scene.

The most radical part of Kesey's education during the Stanford years took place at the Menlo Park VA hospital. A friend told Kesey—who was short of money and had a child on the way—that at the hospital they were paying subjects to ingest psychedelic substances, including LSD ("They" would turn out to be the C.I.A.). Kesey found his initial experiences under the influence of hallucinogenic drugs to be transformative, and so began his love affair with "acid." The VA hospital soon hired him to work the night shift on the psychiatric ward. His work there and his continuing experimentation with

Ken Kesey

LSD inspired *One Flew Over the Cuckoo's Nest*. Written in less than a year during 1961, the book was published in early 1962 to critical acclaim, and went on to enjoy extraordinary and enduring popular success. To date the book has sold over eight million copies. A stage adaptation opened on Broadway in 1964, starring Kirk Douglas and Gene Wilder. In 1975 a hugely popular movie version starring Jack Nicholson won five Academy Awards.

One Flew Over the Cuckoo's Nest was set in a psychiatric ward, pitting a cast of colorful inmates against the castrating Big Nurse Ratched, who represented the brutal fascist system that was the hospital—and by extension, the government. The book, while dark and unsettling, is also thought-provoking, hilarious, and timely. Who is truly crazy in an irrational institution—the inmates or the warders who crush their spirits? Can we, should we trust the people in charge who tell us what to do?

The narrator, six-foot-seven inch Chief Bromden, half native-American, beaten down by the system, pretending to be deaf and mute, believing he is weak and docile, has his consciousness raised by the rebel Randle Patrick McMurphy. At the end of the novel, Chief Bromden realizes his own incredible strength, tears the heavy control panel off the wall, smashes it through the window and escapes. "I remember I was taking huge strides as I ran, seeming to stop and float a long ways before my next foot struck the earth. I felt like I was flying. Free." Within a few years after the publication of *Cuckoo's Nest* many young people would undergo a similar transformation.

The surprising early success of the book allowed Kesey to purchase a tract of land in the tiny town of La Honda in the mountainous forest south of San Francisco. He moved there with his family, and was soon joined by some of his Menlo Park neighbors and other like-minded friends seeking to pursue a nonconformist, psychedelically-enhanced lifestyle. This informal communal group eventually coalesced into the Merry Pranksters. Life at La Honda has been described as a never-ending party, a drug-fueled theater of the absurd where the curtain never came down. Visitor and gonzo journalist Hunter Thompson recalled it as "the world capital of madness. There were no rules, fear was unknown and sleep was out of the question."

Kesey's message in his life and in *Cuckoo's Nest*—to question authority— was an attitude that young Americans were more than ready to embrace as the sixties progressed. Kesey and his Merry Pranksters took it upon them-

Ken Kesey

selves to spread the message in person during their 1964 cross-country trip in the wildly painted school bus named *Further*, a trip that would be immortalized in Tom Wolfe's best selling book, *The Electric Kool-Aid Acid Test*. With a speed-wired Neal Cassady in the driver's seat, the Pranksters stopped often along the way to New York City to mingle with folks, share their drugs and philosophy, perform inspired antics, and generally thumb their noses at whatever manifestations of authority and conformity they encountered.

Despite all the psychedelic hijinks taking place to distract him, at La Honda Kesey managed to complete a second, more ambitious novel, *Sometimes a Great Notion*, in 1963. Published in 1964, it became a resounding success by most authors' standards, selling more than four million copies and receiving high praise from many critics. *Notion* was a sophisticated, multi-generational saga set in Oregon that explored themes of the nature of evil and issues of control: man vs. man, man vs. institution, and man vs. nature. However, it did not achieve the wild popularity and instant cult-like status of his first published book.

Decades later, Kesey would explain in a 1994 interview with the *Paris Review* that he saw his writing, his Prankster experiences, and his other creative acts as different expressions of one life-long performance. "The common denominator is the joker. Tarot scholars say that if it weren't for the fool, the rest of the cards wouldn't exist. The fool in tarot is the naïve innocent spirit with a rucksack over his shoulder, like Kerouac, his eyes up into the sky like Yeats, and his dog biting his rump as he steps over the cliff." The prankster's role is to shake up society; to mock those in power; to point out that the emperor has no clothes. Kesey did that in spades.

So it was that the strapping son of Bible-quoting farmers became first a fine young man of unlimited promise and great charisma and then a leader of the counterculture. In his words, "the bridge" between the beats and the hippies, two of the most subversive youth movements in United States history. Although an idealist who frowned on a culture of empty materialism, he also made his first million before he was thirty. And LSD, the key that helped unlock the door to his fame and fortune, with beautiful irony, had been handed to him by the U.S. government.

DAY ONE

On November 27, 1965, tens of thousands of people marched on Washington, D.C., to protest the war in Vietnam, circling the White House and then rallying in front of the Washington Monument, while on the other side of the country in Santa Cruz, California, a more modest number of people—who would also no doubt be labeled "peaceniks"—were planning to attend a much smaller event that Saturday night. The original hippie movement was hours away from being born. This movement would not be so much about protesting wars, as exploring oneself; equally interested in achieving inner peace as in affecting world peace. It doesn't sound as though a movement dedicated to the nurturing of one's inner self would have much impact beyond its members, but the events in Santa Cruz on November 27, 1965, would ultimately overshadow those taking place in the nation's capital that day.

It is arbitrary to pinpoint the exact moment and place of birth of the hippie movement when it was gestating for years in different locations—the Haight, Virginia City, Nevada, Ken Kesey's Merry Pranksters bus trip across the country, Timothy Leary's psychedelic preachings and experiments in Massachusetts and New York, the Family Dog dances at the Longshoremen's Hall, and when some could argue that the hippies were merely the next stage of evolution after the beats and Neo-Beats, but the first public Acid Test in Santa Cruz was, at the very least, the official announcement of the birth. Since the hippie movement accelerated very quickly after the first Acid Test into more Acid Tests, more light shows, more LSD, more music, more dances, and more sophisticated psychedelic posters, it seems a legitimate starting point. It was the first openly advertised LSD party.

Little remains in the records of these initial acid tests. The most tangible remaining evidence of this pivotal moment is a small poster announcing an "Acid Test" at "Ken Babbs" and featuring "Warlocks."

This hand-made sign was the work of a young man named Norman Hartweg. Some scholars of the hippie movement insist that Jerry Garcia designed the poster, with its squiggly lines and all-seeing Egyptian eye; others maintain that Ken Kesey was responsible or Paul Foster who is credited by some with designing later Acid Test posters. Whatever the case, this modest advertisement would serve as a prototype to the psychedelic poster industry, which was about to burst onto the scene.

Santa Cruz, a small city and university town sixty miles south of San Francisco, was the town closest to Kesey's compound and his best friend Ken Babbs' rural spread. It was becoming the site of a growing community of disaffected young Americans. Two of their popular gathering places, also frequented by the Merry Pranksters, were the Hip Pocket Bookstore and Catalyst Coffee Shop, housed in the same large brick building. It was here at the corner of Pacific Avenue and Front Street that local bohemian and bookstore owner Ron Bevirt—known as Hassler—posted the sign on Saturday morning.

The Egyptian eye sign was certainly cryptic, but those it was intended for got the message. The folks who wanted to take this first acid test knew how to find their way to "Ken Babbs" that evening, even though the venue did not in fact belong to Babbs (who was briefly renting it with his wife, Space Daisy). The birthplace of Hippie, inc.,turned out to be a cavernous barn in rural Scott's Valley, seven or so miles north of Santa Cruz. Built in 1914 and located on a four-hundred-acre farm, it functioned as the Frapwell Dairy Barn until 1948, then served as a community center in the 1950s. Just before the first Acid Test, Eric "Big Daddy" Nord bought the place.

Nord was a San Francisco businessman who planned to turn the Barn into a concert venue for rock bands. He was already associated with a string of clubs and coffee shops, including San Francisco's famed "hungry i" nightclub, where young, up-and-coming entertainers like Barbara Streisand and Bill Cosby performed. First known as the "King of the Beat Generation," Nord made the transition to hippie businessperson. He invited a number of fledgling Bay Area acid and folk/rock bands and singers to perform at the Barn, including Janis Joplin, Quicksilver Messenger Service, Country Joe and the Fish, the Jefferson Airplane, the 13th Floor Elevators, the Lincoln Street Exit, the Burgundy Runn, Captain Beefheart and His Magic Band, and the New Delhi River Band.

The Warlocks, 1965

The featured musical entertainment promoted on the poster for this special evening was a different increasingly popular area band, the Warlocks, led by one Jerry Garcia. Nobody was taking attendance at the Barn on Day One, and there is conflicting literature as to which of the first three Acid Tests the Warlocks played at but we know that as the psychedelic parties evolved, the Warlocks changed their name to The Grateful Dead. Besides Kesey, present at these Acid Tests were both local Santa Cruz residents, students from the just-opened UC Santa Cruz and others from throughout the San

Francisco Bay Area. Neal Cassady and Allen Ginsberg were there, as were a few curious thrill-seekers who had responded to Hassler's sign—"Can You Pass the Acid Test?" Five Santa Cruz Neo-Beats who definitely showed up were Ron Boise, whose 1961 sculpture of a couple engaged in Kama Sutra sex, on display at the Hip Pocket bookstore, set the free-love tone for the hippie movement; Peter Demma, business manager of the Hip Pocket Bookstore and Catalyst Coffee shop; writer Lee Quarnstrom, who lived for a time at the Barn; Space Daisy, who modeled for some of Ron Boise's sculptures; and Ron Bevirt, Hip Pocket owner who helped finance the first public Acid Test. And also there, ready to party as always, were many of the Merry Pranksters.

Burton Wolfe in his book *The Hippies* (1968) provides the earliest description of a public Acid Test when he writes that Kesey hired "The Grateful Dead, rented a garage, and threw a bash for several hundred people. Roy Siebert, a Merry Prankster artist, beamed eerie protoplasmic shapes on the walls with a strobe and movie projector, and one of the first 'light shows' was added to the tests." (Those protoplasmic shapes were a rudimentary version of the more sophisticated folk/rock light shows that Bill Ham was already putting together in Virginia City and at his garage on Pine Street in the Haight.) Within a year of the Acid Tests the folk/rock light show quickly spread nationally and fifty years later, the light show has been adopted by an array of entertainment venues, including the $100 million-plus extravaganza on display worldwide at the opening ceremony of the Beijing Olympics in 2004. Additionally, the light show has become a staple of nearly every type of popular music show, from Goth to Christian to Country Western to Heavy Metal.

Of course, at the end of the first few public Acid Tests, no one knew that the light show would become such a world-wide success. November 27, 1965, generated just a trickle of money from a dilapidated dairy barn and at an alternative bookstore in Santa Cruz, but it marked the beginning of what would become a flood of hippie-generated earnings. LSD would become a multi-million dollar business, psychedelic posters—spurred by a hand-drawn poster —would help pioneer a billion dollar poster industry, and The Grateful Dead would go on to become one of the most celebrated rock bands in history.

Neal Cassady

PART II

✳

THE HIPPIE

BUSINESS WORLD

3

THE HIPPIE
MUSIC BUSINESS

My feeling about the bands of the 60s was that they thought "we are just like you, just like our audience" . . . There was no "fourth wall"— the band was living their lives and we just step up here on the stage— we are getting your (the audience's) permission to play. The stage and the dance floor are equally important. Anybody can do this—you want to do this, just do it—you can express yourself. Here is a guitar, now jump on the stage and play. Many of the musicians came from the hootenanny and folk background—this is a statement that music is a part of life and we were not doing anything special.

—*Mark Braunstein*

THE HIPPIES' INFLUENCE in music is the most well-known artistic and business success story coming out of Haight-Ashbury. Four iconic rock bands lived there: Jerry Garcia and the Grateful Dead, Janis Joplin and Big Brother and the Holding Company, Jefferson Airplane, and Quicksilver Messenger Service. However, almost every popular folk/rock and psychedelic band of the late sixties incorporated hippie styles from dress to hair to album cover art to songs. The hippie influence extended to all the greats from the Beatles to Jimi Hendrix to The Doors to The Who to The Mamas and the Papas to Crosby, Stills, Nash, & Young and on and on.

The Great Society

Haight-Ashbury was also the home—or at least second home—to some of the most successful jazz, blues, folk, country-rock, and classical Indian musicians of the last half of the twentieth-century. These residents included Carlos Santana who, to date, has sold more than 100 million albums; Bobby Hutcherson, a prolific jazz musician (recorded 42 albums as lead musician) and recipient of the lifetime Jazz Master Fellowship Award from the National Endowment for the Arts; Keith Jarrett, an internationally-renowned jazz pianist and composer of the best-selling piano album in music history (The Koln Concert), which sold more than 3.5 million albums; Graham Nash, a world-renowned musician (member of The Hollies and Crosby, Stills, Nash, & Young, who collectively released nearly 100 albums); and Jim Morrison, an internationally-acclaimed musician, and leader of the band The Doors, which sold 32.5 million albums in the U.S.

THE BANDS

Back in 1964, The Beatles appeared on the Ed Sullivan Show. That was an early catalyst for us (me and my band) and for a lot of other people too. So I decided to go into the music business. Richard (Olsen) and Mike (Fergusen) and myself were in North Beach wandering around and we were approached by a gentleman who looked like he had just popped out of the Old West—and he asked us if we were The Byrds. We said no, but we told him that we were a musical group. So we got into a conversation—it seemed serendipitous—we made this contact and followed up with an audition at the Red Dog Saloon in Virginia City and we got the job. We were the first group to perform on LSD due to the fact that the owner of the saloon dosed us all without our knowing it. Well, he thought we sounded great and we got the job—it was a perfect fit. This was the summer of 1965.

—*George Hunter*

In the Haight, the two important catalysts in the transition from folk to folk/rock music were George Hunter, leader of the Charlatans, and native San

The Charlatans

Franciscan Jerry Garcia, a former folk singer whose band the Warlocks would likely have died on the vine had it not been for the Acid Tests and the financial and moral support of Ken Kesey and Augustus Owsley Stanley III (who became the principal supplier of LSD to the hippie world).

As the online music magazine, *Perfect Sound Forever* said, George Hunter and the Charlatans were "so ahead of the times, they were behind the times". They are widely regarded as the first hippie band. In June, a few months before the first public acid party, the Charlatans played at the Red Dog Saloon in Virginia City, Nevada with the first folk/rock light show—designed by Bill Ham—and their own poster. In an interview, George Hunter said that his poster wasn't psychedelic but that it was the granddaddy of posters for the San Francisco music scene. The Charlatans also led the way into hippie fashions.

The Charlatans' look and music played well in Virginia City, an old silver mining town that originated in 1859 with the discovery of the legendary Comstock Lode. Virginia City had attracted American bohemians since the 1930s. In San Francisco, however, by 1966, the band's fame was soon eclipsed by the Jefferson Airplane, the Dead, Big Brother, Quicksilver Messenger Service, the British bands, and others. Though greatly admired, the band seemed out of step with the changes happening in San Francisco in 1966 and 1967, and it wasn't long before they broke up. George Hunter, who founded the group, had a great visual sense and was responsible for the band's eye-catching outfits. He left the band in 1968 and went on to design album covers.

Though the distinctive dress and musical styles George Hunter and the Charlatans originated set the musical tone and fashion style of the Haight-Ashbury bohemians in the weeks leading up to November 27, 1965, it took Jerry Garcia and his two bands to bring early hippie music to national attention and acclaim, while the Charlatans would fade from memory.

> People think Jerry was just a rock singer, but before the Warlocks, he was an early sixties folk singer and cantoneer in the style of Bob Dylan and Woody Guthrie. Once the Dead began, he became something different—he constructed a genre that was a combination of Dylan's folk music and standard rock. I knew Jerry personally, lived next door

The Grateful Dead, 1966

Jerry Garcia

to him. Many think he was a goofball, but that was just a show. Jerry was also an extremely serious musician and a damned good business-man, too

—*Tsvi Strauch*

Within months of Day One, many young people around the world began rocking to the eclectic, folk, rock, bluesy music the Grateful Dead helped originate. The Dead inspired such passion in thousands that they became not just fans but followers, who called themselves Deadheads and followed the band from gig to gig around the country and the world. Although all band members were beloved, Garcia was their unquestioned leader and the force behind their remarkable, enduring success.

"Jerry was an intellectual—a student of art, music, and history," says Mark Braunstein. "There was a lot of depth to him that his fans never saw."

The Grateful Dead sold over thirty-five million albums and played live to over twenty-five million people. They also made millions of dollars from their intellectual property and merchandising rights—one of the few rock' n roll pioneers to retain ownership of their music masters and publishing permissions.

ENTREPRENEURS

Like "Big Daddy" Nord, Frank Werber, Bill Graham and Chet Helms weren't professional musicians but were important elements in the hippie music business. They were the entrepreneurs who together with the artists created the buzz and the billion dollar folk/rock industry.

An Austrian Jew, Frank Werber escaped a Nazi prison camp with his father during the war, fleeing to the United States. After high school, Frank joined the Navy, becoming a midshipman and sharpshooter. After attending the American Academy of Art in Chicago and the University of Colorado, he wound up in San Francisco, where he became manager of the hungry i, the famed North Beach nightclub. There he discovered his calling as a manager/promoter.

> Werber preceded all the hippie folk/rock bands when he managed the 'folkies,' particularly, the Lamplighters. Werber also managed an enormously successful group called The Kingston Trio, who played music that was a blend of pop and folk music that really appealed to the sock hop set. Then he managed a psychedelic folk singer named Malachi. So you can see that Werber's first two bands were pre-psychedelic and Malachi was dead-on psychedelic. Werber nailed it every time! He became one of the first rich long-haired businessmen managing these hugely successful singing groups.
>
> —Tsvi Strauch

Another refugee, Bill Graham, was placed by his mother in a Berlin orphanage to help protect him from the Nazis. The children in the orphanage eventually went to France and when France fell to the Germans the Jewish orphans marched across the Pyrenees to Spain. Many of them died along the way. Later, as an American youth, Bill was honored for acts of heroism in combat, receiving both a Bronze Star and a Purple Heart for his outstanding service in the Korean War. Beneath the hippie label he was a tough guy and an ambitious entrepreneur. According to Jay Thelin:

> Bill Graham got his start by managing fund raising concerts for the S.F. Mime Troupe. He also managed the first Trips Festival for Ken Kesey and the Pranksters. Ron and I were given permission to set up a small booth at the Trips Festival announcing the opening of the Psychedelic Shop. We were back stage setting up the booth and there was a loud banging on one of the emergency exit doors from the outside. I went over and opened the door and it was Bill Graham with a shopping bag full of money. He was simply moving the money to a safer place because the crowds were overwhelming and remember, at the Trips Festival, there was Acid in the Kool Aid. It was here that he might have gotten the idea that a lot of money could be made promoting concerts.

Bill Ham tells a similar but slightly different version of Bill Graham's epiphany. "At the Trips Festival, Kesey was at the back door letting people in for free while Graham was at the front door charging a dollar to get in. That was when he supposedly saw the light and decided to build a lucrative career in the music concert business."

Bill Graham's Fillmore became one of the two main venues in San Francisco for all of the great bands of the 1960s. In stark contrast to fellow promoter Frank Werber, Bill was as "anti-drug" as a Baptist minister, and he was extremely clear, although not particularly successful, about forbidding people to use drugs at his concerts. In his autobiography, he states that he ingested LSD only one time, and that was only because someone slipped it to him.

Graham lived a full life which ended unexpectedly in 1991 when he died on a stormy night in a helicopter crash on his way home from a Huey Lewis

Bill Graham

Chet Helms

concert at The Concord Pavilion, north of Berkeley. Fittingly, the Grateful Dead, among other bands, played at his memorial service at Golden Gate Park in San Francisco. An estimated 300,000 people turned out.

The other great hippie promoter was Chet Helms. He was a small-town Texas teenager who liked to talk philosophy in high school—the proverbial square peg. After trying a year in a Texas college, Helms hightailed it to San Francisco where he eventually joined up with another Texas kid who didn't quite fit in—Janis Joplin.

More prolific than Werber and Graham, Helms was involved in approximately 105 business collaborations. He formed Family Dog Productions which grew from the Family Dog commune (founded by Ellen Harmon and Luria Castell). Along with Bill Graham, Chet Helms spearheaded the folk/rock musical explosion that was just beginning. The Fillmore Auditorium and the Avalon Ballroom where they promoted their concerts dominated the San Francisco music scene.

There were other important music places in San Francisco such as The Western Front and the Carousel Ballroom, but none of the others were able to sustain themselves. Why? Tsvi Strauch sums it up: "Bill and Chet had all the famous bands sewed up—they were brilliant in that way."

As competitors, there was sometimes tension between them. John Helms, Chet's brother, offered, in an interview, a personal perspective on these two dominant musical promoters.

> There definitely were conflicts in terms of their styles—Bill was a New York businessman and with Chet, it was not about the money. Chet was very spiritual, a true mystic. We both knew that we were living in interesting times. Chet saw the concerts as a tribal event in which young males and females of the species came together and met each other and that was a part of it. I guess you could say that with Chet, the concerts were tribal gatherings and with Bill, it was about making money. Their philosophies were at odds with each other, but don't misunderstand, they thought very much of each other and both men expressed this appreciation to each other.

The distinctive folk/rock style of the hippie bands became an overnight sensation. Werber, Graham and Helms generated for themselves and their

Members of the Grateful Dead and New Riders of the Purple Sage

clients hundreds of millions of dollars. Collectively the three men had their promotional hands on the payouts of dozens of successful bands as well as the careers of highly successful writers and entertainers, including the Rolling Stones, the Doors, Neil Young, Bob Dylan, Crosby, Stills and Nash; Blood, Sweat & Tears; Frank Zappa, Lovin' Spoonful; and Bo Diddley. For many, however, it wasn't just about the music, but about the ambiance, too.

AMBIANCE

The use of electrical lights and images in theater may be traced back to the 1920s when European set constructors designed light-projected backdrops for various scenes, eliminating the time-consuming and laborious task of moving props off and on the stage. Modern-day light shows are connected mainly to three people: Seymour Locks, an art professor at San Francisco State University, and artists Elias Romero and Bill Ham. Professor Locks first created the light show effect in the early fifties by placing a small wristwatch face filled with paint on the lens of a standard classroom transparent overhead projector. Projecting a nondescript image onto a screen, Locks altered the abstract images by stirring the paint or tipping the watch face to create a continuously changing display of images.

Art student Elias Romero learned the Locks technique and began his own performances, spreading the word about this new art form. He loaned a projector to Bill Ham whose light shows transported Locks' invention from the classroom to the world stage. His kinetic art provided a performance environment that enveloped the space and the audience for some of the most noted concerts of the hippie movement and San Francisco music scene of the 1960s. For the Red Dog Saloon Bill invented a light panel that responded to sounds, creating an infinite number of colors and forms. At the Avalon theater there were no fixed seats, the audience participated in the art—they were dancing to the music and the light. (The audience/the dancers, were not passive listeners but were important active players in the hippie music experience.) Bill also started his own theater, the Light Sound Dimension (LSD)

Members of the
Family Dog
commune

Ellen Harmon, one
of the founders of
the Family Dog
Commune

theater where jazz musicians and Bill using a transparent overhead projector would improvise electric light-sound art creating what the San Francisco Chronicle's music and art critic Alfred Frankenstein said was the only theater of its kind in the world.

In 1970 Ham moved to Europe for three years where he presented a performance of Electric Action painting at the Museum of Modern Art in Paris as well as other performances in France and Switzerland. Some of these performances were with tapes from the Light Sound Dimension and other times with live jazz musicians. All of the performances were improvised continuous creations.

Bill Ham grew up in the Mississippi Delta during the 1930s. He graduated with an art degree from the University of Houston and shortly thereafter, enlisted in the army. Serving in Europe during the Korean War, he took every opportunity to visit some of the greatest museums of the world, particularly in Berlin and Rome. After his time of service, he arrived in San Francisco in 1958, interested in joining the beat movement. He took up residence at a large boarding house on Pine Street—a providential move.

> In the early 1960s, the North Beach scene spilled out of the neighborhood because of the necessity for cheaper rent and one of the nearest places was Pine Street and, specifically, 2111 Pine Street, which was the address of a large rooming house. Everyone in the house shared a kitchen and several bathrooms, and this eventually became the address of The Family Dog commune.
>
> —*Bill Ham*

His recollections of this legendary house helps us understand not only the beginning of light shows but the days leading up to the hippie movement.

> During this early time (1963, 1964), the neighborhood (Pine Street area) was the immediate audience (for light shows). We would open the garage door and the neighbors would enter. We would close the door and do the show. The door would open and the audience would spill out. These were some of the very earliest light shows. The first light show that was connected to rock-and-roll in a big way was the

Trips Festival in January 1966. That was when all the different art groups participated in this great art and music happening. Kesey had been busted again and publicity about him began to grow. The Trips Festival, took place at the Longshoremen's Hall and was totally disorganized. We were all startled to see how many people showed up.

Today, 82-year old Bill Ham, a proud grandfather, lives in an old San Francisco Victorian, not far from the old Pine Street neighborhood, where he spends his days creating art which he sells online.

POSTER ARTISTS

When Norman Hartweg, Army veteran and University of Michigan graduate, put pen to paper on the morning of November 27,1965 to advertise the first public Acid Test, little did he know that this simple poster combined with George Hunter's Charlatans poster would help ignite a billion-dollar industry. These posters were followed by hundreds of psychedelic posters advertising Family Dog concerts, the Jefferson Airplane, Avalon Ballroom and Fillmore Auditorium events, Janis Joplin, Big Brother and the Holding Company, Bob Dylan, The Doors, and many more. Stapled to the telephone poles and doorways of Haight-Ashbury, later ripped off and tossed into trash bins, some of the posters that managed to survive those times now sell for thousands of dollars.

Though Hartweg's poster contained some of the rudimentary design elements, it was hippie graphic artist Wes Wilson who has been credited for inventing the psychedelic art motif. Wilson together with four more hippie artists shot psychedelic posters and the psychedelic motif into a commercial stratosphere: Wes Wilson, Alton Kelley, Victor Moscoso, Rick Griffin and Stan Miller were known as, the San Francisco Five. They produced 160 posters for Family Dog Productions concert events. In conjunction with legendary concert promoters Chet Helms and Bill Graham, they made some of the most memorable posters of the era to advertise some of history's greatest rock concerts.

The San Francisco Five: Alton Kelley, Victor Moscoso,
Rick Griffin, Wes Wilson, Stan Miller

Once the psychedelic art motif caught on with other designers it was soon adopted by the likes of General Motors, Neiman Marcus, and Campbell's Soup. The motif influenced the work of designers in the advertising industry and product development worldwide for years to come.

Besides posters, Victor Moscoso also created art for album covers, t-shirts and Zap Comix and is still a working artist. Stanley Miller, Jr. (also known as "Mouse") was a Detroit-born artist who deftly combined artistic talent with business acumen. As a teenager, he started a mail order company (with the help of his parents) to sell his work and designed the Superfuzz character which was enormously popular with kids in the early and mid-1960s. He then moved to Haight-Ashbury, opened Mouse Studios at 1711 Haight Street, and a year later, started the Berkeley Bonaparte Distribution Agency along with his fellow San Francisco Five artists and began creating the great concert posters. Mouse added t-shirts to his repertoire in 1969 and his most popular graphic t-shirts featured the Grateful Dead and images of marijuana plants and pot culture. The graphic-t—dominated by Disney characters in the 1950s (neither Mickey Mouse nor Davy Crockett appealed to rebellious teens)—became an enduring and ubiquitous symbol of youthful revolt in the 1960s with newly invented printing techniques mastered by Mouse and other hippie graphic artists.

By the age of twenty-four, Mouse had already established himself as a premiere American screen-printer. Thus, in this single hippie businessman/artist, we see a pioneer of not one, but two billion-dollar industries: screen-printed posters and screen-printed graphic tees.

Del Renzio spotted his genius back in the early Haight days, as he wrote in *The Flower Children*: "Mouse is almost an archetypal hippie, hairily bizarre, eyes that spring constantly to a sparkle behind steel-rimmed spectacles, emphasizing an oblique irony, while sensitive hands frequently gesture the warmth he feels towards his fellows. He is happiest when he has no money, and with his talent this is a pretty difficult achievement."

Another poster artist that needs to be mentioned is Bonnie MacLean. She was one of the first female hippie poster artists and created some of the most beautiful posters of the 60s. Like any of the hippie women who became successful her achievements are that much more impressive because the hippie culture, while progressive in many ways, was backward in its treatment of women. Hippie culture was male dominated, some would say misogynistic.

When Bonnie was in second grade in Trenton, New Jersey, her teacher hung on the classroom display wall a drawing Bonnie had made of her grandmother. "Zap, the lightbulb went on, and it stayed on through all the years it took me to get to becoming an image maker," she said in an interview. Reaching her goal came about circuitously. She always loved school and graduated from Penn State in 1961 with a B.A. in liberal arts, with a major in French. As much as she wanted to be an image maker, she had no idea how to be that and make a living.

She worked at Allis-Chalmers Machine Company where she met Bill Graham. She became first his secretary, then his wife. When he left Allis-Chalmers to manage the San Francisco Mime troupe and then became a rock impresario at the Fillmore Auditorium she was always in the background doing a lot of the grunt work.

The Haight: A Russian Immigrant Community

I was a jack-of-all-trades: secretary, selling tickets, anything that needed to be done. And I eventually became in charge of the "Coming Attractions" board which advertised upcoming concerts. That is where I got my chops for the poster making.

—*Bonnie MacLean*

When Wes Wilson and Bill had a falling out over money Bonnie added poster-making to her Fillmore tasks, finally fulfilling her second grade dream of being an "image maker." Like many of the original hippies she was unafraid to take risks and worked long hours, needing to turn out a new poster every week. At first she just imitated Wes but after much practice she felt more confident and developed her own artistic style. She helped Bill grow the Fillmore business and created museum quality posters that have appeared in exhibitions across the country from the San Francisco's Museum of Modern Art to MOMA in New York. She is still a practicing artist today.

Bonnie and the San Francisco Five were part of a larger group of hippie poster artists and print shops that transformed not only concert posters but product advertising and album covers, which until the hippies had been somewhat pedestrian. As the hippie aesthetic gained influence album covers became more colorful and artistic.

The hippie artists tinkered with Offset Lithography—a complicated mechanical process—which had dominated commercial printing for decades. Working in collaboration with small creative print shops they figured out new sophisticated ways of using the equipment and expanding its capabilities. Their techniques and color manipulations paved the road for modern graphic software like Adobe Photoshop and Illustrator.

The hippies were also involved in the distribution of their products. One of the main publishers and distributors of screen printed and photo-offset posters in the U.S. was the Print Mint located in Berkeley and the Haight. Many of the most popular posters sold there were designed by the aforementioned "San Francisco Five" and other hippie artists.

The hippie poster artists were creative and talented and also lucky that four things that often contribute to innovation success were at play: technology, product innovation, effective distribution, and early adoption by a sizable group of eager consumers with financial means. New technology (inventive use of flat multi-color and split fountain rainbow inking effects) combined with wholly original and appealing artistic product design (the psychedelic motif), an effective means to distribute product (relatively easy transportability, in conjunction with distribution hubs, like the Print Mint,) in demand by a large and expanding market of young and affluent American consumers, together were conducive to the rapid diffusion of this innovation. They were also lucky to have creative and bold print shops attuned to their art.

OUTCOME

Billions flowed from the folk-rock and psychedelic albums, concerts, posters and light shows. Five decades later hippie music is still popular. One station on Sirius radio plays only songs from The Grateful Dead. Light shows keep expanding into more entertainment venues. Psychedelic posters are collector's items. In the music business and other industries the hippies saw what others didn't. They were open to the future and a different way and they helped create that way.

4

MONEY

THE DEATH OF MONEY

FROM THE BEGINNING there were oppositional forces within the hippie culture. Making money was more important to some hippies than others. The Diggers according to Judith Goldhaft, one of the original Diggers:

> left the San Francisco Mime Troupe to move into the streets of San Francisco and create a form of political street theater that relied on Life-Acting. . . . The Digger motto was, 'Everything is free; do your own thing.' In general the Diggers helped provide the basic necessities such as food, shelter, medical care and clothing freely so that people could explore social interactions and pursue their preferred lifestyles. The Diggers provided free events in the parks and streets and ran Free Stores at several locations in the Haight-Ashbury, where all products were literally free. They celebrated anonymity and were anti-authoritarian, anti-industrial mechanization, anti-media manipulation, and anti-consumerism.

The Diggers named themselves after the seventeenth century English Diggers who envisioned a world free from buying, selling, and private property. Like many of the other counter-culture inhabitants of Haight-Ashbury they did not see themselves as hippies. They were often at odds with the hippie merchants.

One of the founders of the Diggers, Brooklyn-born and bred, restless and rebellious, Emmett Grogan was at times openly hostile to the merchants. Emmett had dropped out of Duke University after a year and showed up in the Haight, where he made a memorable impact. His persona often was that of a New York street gangster and several merchants felt they might be physically harmed if they didn't turn their shops into nonprofit cooperatives.

> Grogan and some of the Diggers would come to our meetings demanding that we pay them money to help them feed the street people. So we would give them money to get them off our backs—you know, pay them off, so we could get back to doing business without being hassled. It was like a mob shake-down.
>
> —*Tsvi Strauch*

Fellow Digger and Hollywood actor Peter Coyote later described Grogan as "extreme and contradictory, quarrelsome and kind, charismatic and self-destructive, who willed himself to be a hero." Although some regarded him as self-mythologizing, Grogan's contributions to Hippie, inc., are real. The Diggers introduced the concept of "free" stores, gave away free bread, which reintroduced whole grain breads back into the American diet—creating a new industry—and their free clothing included tie-dye fabrics which was part of a hippie fashion revolution.

The Diggers were also quite the phrase makers. At least two epigrams credited to them have become so popular as to be almost clichés. Though Emmett sometimes took credit for these sayings, it was actually other Diggers who coined them: Peter Berg for *Do your Own Thing* and Gregory Corso for *Today is the first day of the rest of your life*. Had these epigrams been copyrighted and licensed, the Diggers would have netted millions of dollars.

Emmett Grogan died on a New York subway platform on April 6, 1978 at the age of thirty-five. According to Peter Coyote, the cause was a heroin overdose. At the time of his death—ten years after the Diggers declared "the death of money" in Haight-Ashbury—Grogan lived in an upscale New York City penthouse with his actress wife and their son.

Diggers celebrating victory at the courthouse: (left to right) Le Mortadella, Emmett Grogan, Slim Minnaux, Peter Berg, and Butcher Brooks

THE HIGH OF MONEY

Look at my photographs from those days and look at the faces and eyes. What you see, what I see, is acid. Every one of them—you see LSD in their faces.

—*Herb Greene*

Augustus Owsley Stanley III was the scion of a powerful Kentucky political family. His grandfather was a U.S. senator from 1903 to 1915 and governor of Kentucky from 1915 to 1919. Augustus Owsley Stanley I was considered one of the most progressive politicians of his time, taking on the likes of U.S. Steel and American Tobacco. In death, he is also distinguished as the

Acid at Human Be-In

grandfather of the most successful maker and seller of pure LSD in the mid-sixties.

Owsley III was an inventor known by several names, including Bear and LSD Millionaire, but most hippies just called him Owsley. He worked at times as the sound engineer for The Grateful Dead. He was an expert in miking for live recordings and his skill was highly valued and utilized by Jefferson Airplane, Janis Joplin, Santana, Jimi Hendrix, Johnny Cash, and Miles Davis. He had been an electronics and radar specialist for the U.S. Air Force, trained in ballet, fluent in Russian, a 1963 Berkeley drop-out. In addition to his technical expertise he was a skilled chemist: he was the principal supplier of LSD to Ken Kesey and the Haight-Ashbury hippies during the hundred-week period of the original hippie movement. Owsley's LSD was purportedly finer and purer than others, and he devised a way to produce it in huge quantities, dominating the market to such an extent that the *Oxford English Dictionary* contains an entry for the noun Owsley as "an extremely potent, high-quality type of LSD." He also employed a marketing technique referred to as "freetail," that today is particularly favored by Internet and direct marketers, who entice people to their sites by offering to give them their product free of charge. As

Acid at Human Be-In

Tsvi Strauch recalls: "Whenever Owsley would cook up a new batch of acid he would give a bunch of it to Chet Helms who would hand it out free to the people attending the music show that night at the Avalon Ballroom. It was a clever technique that served to introduce thousands to LSD."

Between 1965 and 1967, Owsley manufactured an estimated 1.25 million doses of LSD. According to *San Francisco Chronicle* columnist Joel Selvin, Owsley is "the most famous brand name in LSD history." Besides his name becoming synonymous with the product he sold, his contributions to Hippie, inc., include using his millions to finance a burgeoning folk-rock music industry.

Rock Skully and
Tangerine sitting on
hood of car. George
Hunter standing with
back to camera.

LSD—Lysergic acid diethylamide—was developed by Sandoz Laboratories in Switzerland in 1938 by a chemist named Dr. Albert Hofmann. Acid was fully legal in the early sixties when Timothy Leary and Richard Alpert (who later changed his name to Ram Das) began experimenting with LSD and other psychedelics at Harvard. Allen Ginsberg joined them and began a campaign of introducing the drugs to other intellectuals and artists hoping they would discover a higher level of consciousness (an independent campaign already had begun among the scientists in the Menlo Park area). When LSD made its way to the streets of San Francisco in 1964, it was still legal. California made it illegal in October 1966. The rest of the nation followed two years later.

Within days of LSD being declared illegal, thirty-one-year-old Ken Kesey publicly denounced the drug, not because he believed that it was bad for people, but because he didn't want himself or anyone else to land in jail. By then, at least one hippie entrepreneur—Owsley—had made his fortune.

It was not until the mid-seventies that the Central Intelligence Agency revealed that during the fifties and sixties it had been running a secret project, code-named MKULTRA, to experiment with manipulating people's mental states. The extensive—and illegal—program, conducted through more than thirty universities, hospitals, federal prisons and other institutions, included administering LSD to unwitting volunteers in uncontrolled dosages and settings, observed by unqualified CIA agents.

This cynical experimenting on American citizens proved disastrous for some participants. We may never know its full impact. There is one documented death; untold others found themselves affected for life. One subject was Boston's notorious gangster James "Whitey" Bulger, who volunteered for the MKULTRA program as a young prisoner at Alcatraz in return for a reduced sentence. He claimed that after his LSD trips he was never able to sleep through a single night again.

For Ken Kesey, exposure to LSD through the MKULTRA program proved revelatory rather than mind-destroying, and marked the beginning of his decades-long use of the drug. Unlike many of the CIA's unsuspecting subjects, he was particularly well-prepared for the prolonged sensory bombardment that a trip involves. As he told the *Paris Review* in 1993.

By the time I started taking peyote and LSD, I had already done a great deal of reading about mysticism—the *Bhagavad Gita* and Zen and Christian mystical texts. They helped me to interpret what I was seeing, to give it meaning. You don't just take the stuff and expect understanding. It is also important not to be in a hellish place with LSD or it can be a hellish experience. You need to be in a secure setting.

Tsvi Strauch explained the interactive relationship between the hippies and LSD.

How did the LSD trip connect to the hippie movement? The music and the art all strengthened, the spiritual, inward journey—these things got stronger. Yoga, meditation, self-awareness, consciousness, awareness of the importance of the body—that the body was the temple of God and that the right food is needed. This all came out of the experience of the trip. If my body is the temple of God, then I want to give my body the very best. I want to eat clean food, organic, natural, what is the very best for my temple.

When you are at the center of your trip, it is just you and the universe and so you wonder where did the idea of government and authority and the state come from. You question authority—this is a natural outcome of the trip. To not be afraid to be who you are, to be without any restriction from society, to move beyond how you were socialized as a child—and this makes you question authority. The acid trips provoked us to question the Vietnam War and to oppose it.

Nudity was pretty superfluous. True, some people would strip at the concerts and festivals, but it wasn't like people were walking naked down Haight Street. The nudity, though, came out of the LSD trip—people wanted to be unfettered, free. Torn jeans and tie-dye shirts came about through experimentation, attempts to decorate one's clothing with embroidery and spiritual symbols. The Native American and western look was a hippie attempt to return to our natural roots. The desire to go natural grew out of the trip.

For those who haven't drunk the Kool-Aid it may be difficult to balance the notion of the body as a temple and the ingestion of psychedelic drugs. Some adherents like Ken Kesey and Steve Jobs believed they gained insight from taking the drug, and others experienced LSD psychosis and were left mad, either temporarily or, in some cases, forever. The scientific literature indicates that a person's reaction to LSD will depend on many factors: the strength of the dose, one's current state of mind, the other people present, and other drugs recently ingested.

While a person's experience on acid is highly individual, there are some recognizable patterns. Those who *repeatedly* drop acid, and don't suffer obvious harmful effects, predictably develop similar preferences and/or attitudes:

* a preference for natural over synthetic
* a prioritizing of feelings and personal experience over emotional detachment from the dictates of social norms and good taste
* emotional transparency versus interpersonal game-playing
* a placing of perception on equal footing with reality
* an embrace of the divine and supernatural
* the belief that there are many ways to discover truth
* a view that assigns more importance to the process than the outcome
* a stance suspicious of anything declared authoritative or anyone claiming to be the final authority

These eight attitudes, born directly from the experience of dropping acid, became some of the central tenets of hippie philosophy, the conceptual framework for several hippie ideas and preferences like organic gardening, psychedelic art, graphic and tie-dyed clothing, modern evangelical Christian worship styles, and gender-bending unisex fashions. American consumer tastes over the last five decades have been formed not only by New York "Mad Men," but by Haight-Ashbury youth, too—minds that were frequently brilliant and totally blown.

Carlos Santana

Ron McKernan
(Pigpen)

THE SCENT OF MONEY

My dad, who was born in Puerto Rico, said plants had to have purpose; they either fed your sense of taste, your sense of smell or your sense of enjoyment.

—*Jeanne Rose*

Jeanne Rose is a living legend in the aromatherapy world who also made her mark in fashion during the first years of the hippie movement. She is a perfect ambassador for Hippie, inc., embodying the intelligence, creativity, work ethic, entrepreneurial spirit, respect for the natural world, and principled and authentic living that characterized much of the original hippie movement. She started life on an apricot farm in California. Her dad grew whatever the family needed. He was born in Puerto Rico and met Jeanne's mom, who was French Canadian, via an early predecessor of online dating—a lovelorn section of a New York newspaper. He wrote, she wrote, he wrote, she wrote . . . and six weeks later she was on a cross-country bus to meet and get married.

When Jeanne was 11, she was already showing signs that she would be highly accomplished in whatever interested her. With dreams of being an Olympic swimmer and diver she traveled by herself on a 100-mile roundtrip bus ride twice a week to the Crystal Plunge Pool on Lombard Street in San Francisco, where the future Hall of Fame coach, Charlie Sava, was consistently winning national championships. When she took up smoking at 13, her Olympic hopes faded. As a "nerdy science major" in college she received a full scholarship to the University of Miami Marine Laboratory. After graduating she had a job doing field studies of insects and bugs for an Agricultural Experiment Station in Florida but she hated Florida and moved back to California. There she made a life-changing visit to Big Sur, staying at a cabin at the top of a hill, with no electricity or plumbing. She moved in and her world shifted instantly and dramatically. To provide for herself and her child, she started sewing clothes and became a successful fashion designer, creating one-of -a kind high quality clothes. In 1965, she founded New Age Creations, which then was a clothier making organically designed 100% pure cotton, wool, linen and silk garments.

> I designed and made clothes for various members of many "Rock 'n Roll" groups. I worked under various names including Jeanne Colon, Jean Rose, Jeanne the Tailor and finally Jeanne Rose. These groups included Big Brother & The Holding Company, Charles Lloyd Band (Keith Jarrett, Jack deJohnnette, Ron McClure, Charles Lloyd), . . . Country Joe & the Fish (Barry Melton and others), Donovan, Elvin Bishop, Everly Brothers . . . Grateful Dead, Jefferson Airplane (Jorma Kaukonen, Jack Casady, Grace Slick), Paul Butterfield Band, Quicksilver Messenger Service, Steve Miller Band (Tim Davis), Young Rascals and many others including band managers, groupies, roadies, and even hangers-on.
>
> —*Jeanne Rose,* **Reflections of a Hippie Chic**

Around this time she became interested in aromatherapy and by 1968 her company evolved into the first aromatherapy body care company in the U.S. Jean's mother had passed on to her the values of self-motivation and self-education. "I could do these things and I didn't need to ask anybody for praise. It was me, I needed to please me."

Like Owsley, she was an early player, a pioneer in a new industry. Using only organic ingredients she created and dominated the early natural body-care and cosmetics market. In 1969 she wrote the first modern book of Herbalism, *Herbs & Things*, which has sold over 600,000 copies. She has since written over twenty books, including *The Herbal Body Book*, *The Aromatherapy Book*, and *Jeanne Rose's Herbal Guide to Food*.

Jeanne has taught herbs, aromatherapy and distillation throughout the U.S. She organized the aromatherapy industry and became the president of the National Association of Holistic Aromatherapy and later the president of the American Herbalist Association. In the present day she serves as Executive Director of The Aromatic Plant Project, which continues her interest in preserving the natural world and supporting American agriculture.

Like many of the original hippies entrepreneurs Jeanne built her businesses based on her passions and values and strong work ethic. In 1980 she gave away her company, New Age Creations, to her employees and worked as a consultant to other companies developing skin care and body care products and perfumes. Still going strong in her eighth decade, still working —teaching and creating and selling aromatherapy and herbal studies courses—she still lives a life infused with many of the same values of her hippie days.

> My work is not done—there is still so much to do. I think that the more people learn about plants the more they will want to make their own perfume and in the learning they will become more responsible and educated about the environment and realize that "nature" provides.
>
> —*Jeanne Rose*

THE MONEY NETWORK

> Stewart (Brand) was the first one to get it. He was the first person to understand cyberspace. He was the one who coined the term personal computer. And he influenced an entire generation, including an entire generation of technologists.
>
> —*John Markoff*, **What the Dormouse Said: How the Sixties Counter-Culture Shaped the Personal Computer Industry**

In *The Electric Kool-Aid Acid Test*, Tom Wolfe's bestselling book about Ken Kesey and his band of Merry Pranksters' wild bus trip across the country— fueled by hallucinogenic drugs and a desire to confront the banality of the establishment—there is a description on page 2 of a man wearing a blazing disk on his forehead, no shirt, and "a whole necktie made of Indian Beads . . . on bare skin and a white butcher's coat with medals from the King of Sweden on it." Beneath that idiosyncratic exterior was a brilliant visionary who after graduating from Stanford University and serving in the U.S. army infantry, researched for and performed in a multi-media show—"America Needs Indians"—in the sixties, and was one of the producers of the 1966 San Francisco Trips Festival, an all-night rock 'n' roll and light show extravaganza, which helped launch the folk/rock music business. Two years later Stewart Brand put together the *Whole Earth Catalogue*—which won a National Book Award, and that Apple founder Steve Jobs described as "Google in paperback form, thirty-five years before Google came along." In that same year, he assisted Douglas Englebart with his famous presentation of new computer technologies, "The Mother of all Demos"—which included hypertext, video conferencing, e-mail, and the mouse, decades before most of these technologies became part of our everyday lives. In 1974 he conceptualized and wrote about personal computers—two years before Apple Computer started up and seven years before IBM introduced its first PC—and then in 1985 six years before Tim Berners-Lee created the World Wide Web, Brand was a partner in an online computer conferencing center: The WELL—Whole Earth 'Lectronic Link. Founded by Brand and Larry Brilliant, WELL helped create what *Wired* magazine called, "the world's most influential online community," and *Time* magazine said, "WELL was a precursor of every online business from Amazon.com to eBay."

Being ahead of his time is part of Brand's *modus operandi*. He edited the *CoEvolution Quarterly* and together with its staff and the staff of the *Whole Earth Software Catalogue* they put together the first hacker's conference, linking computer hackers with the Whole Earth community. This pattern of networking and integrating the counterculture with technology is a theme throughout Brand's life and career. In the book from *Counterculture to Cyberculture (Stewart Brand, the Whole Earth Network, and the Rise of Digital Utopianism)* the author, Fred Turner, asks, "How was it, then, that computers and computer networks became linked to visions of peer to peer ad-hocracy, a leveled marketplace, and a more authentic self? Where did these visions come from? And who enlisted computing machines to represent them?" He then goes on to answer his questions:

> An extraordinarily influential group of San Francisco Bay area journalists and entrepreneurs: Stewart Brand and the Whole Earth network. Between the late 1960s and the late 1990s, Brand assembled a network of people and publications that together brokered a series of encounters between bohemian San Francisco and the emerging technology hub of Silicon Valley to the south. . . Throughout the late 1980s and

Stewart Brand

early 1990s, Brand and other members of the network, including Kevin Kelly, Howard Rheingold, Esther Dyson, and John Perry Barlow, became some of the most-quoted spokespeople for a counter-cultural vision of the Internet. In 1993 all would help create the magazine that, more than any other, depicted the emerging digital world in revolutionary terms: *WIRED*.

Further linking the philosophies of the counter culture to technology and to business, Brand was also one of the founders of the Global Business Network. GBN networked artists, musicians, scientists and some of the largest corporations and organizations in the world including IBM, AT&T, Royal Dutch Shell, and the Pentagon.

Growing up in Rockford, Illinois, the son of an MIT trained engineer and Vassar educated mom, Stewart inherited his mother's interest in Space. One of his favorite books was *The Conquest of Space* with illustrated images of possible future exploration of the solar system. Like many future hippies he also grew up with a fear of nuclear annihilation. A list had been circulated that had Rockford, because of its machine tools industry, as the seventh most likely city to be hit by an atomic bomb. Fred Turner quotes Stewart saying, "I had a nightmare—one of those horrible, vivid, never forget nightmares—there was chaos and then I looked around and I was the only person left alive in Rockford—a knee-high creature."

Luckily, there was no annihilation, Stewart Brand grew tall, and appeared everywhere, from the Hayden Planetarium, to the New York art world and the art troupe USCO, to petitioning NASA to release a picture of the whole earth, to designing and organizing "The New Games Tournament," to an advisor to California Governor Jerry Brown, to co-founder of The Long Now Foundation fostering long-term responsibility, to an advisor to Eco Trust preserving temperate rain forests from Alaska to San Francisco, to board member of The Santa Fe Institute and The Electronic Frontier Foundation, to visiting scientist at the MIT Media Lab, to Ken Kesey and to Newt Gingrich. From left to right, and everywhere in the middle of the counter-culture and digital revolutions, Brand was there, writing books, trying to preserve the planet, and networking along the way as he helped to shape and define and grandfather the lucrative wired world.

THE DIVERSITY OF MONEY

Emmett Grogan, Owsley, Jeanne Rose, and Stewart Brand form a microcosm that reflects the hippies' broad and varied relationship to money. Much of what Emmett and the Diggers accomplished centered around the free stores and free medical clinics. Emmett criticized the commercialization of the hippies. Owsley was a creative and brilliant capitalist inventor. He gave away some of his products for free, and he financially helped the Oracle, the Diggers, and struggling bands, but he had no qualms about making money from his inventions. Jeanne followed her talents and passions, created businesses, wrote books, lectured all over the world and made and lost money and gave away her business to her employees. Money was always a secondary consideration to her beliefs and values. Stewart Brand, like Jeanne, followed his passions and brilliance wherever it led. He dramatically influenced the culture staying true to his values and while he made some money in many fields over several decades from his ideas and work ethic, personal wealth creation wasn't his goal. Yet he was a pioneer in a digital industry that is now worth trillions.

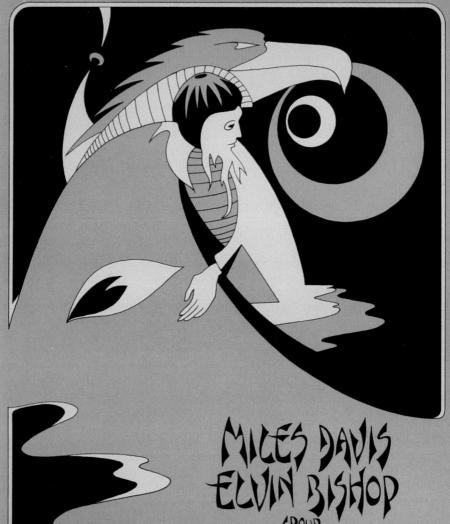

MILES DAVIS
ELVIN BISHOP
GROUP
MANDRILL
LIGHTS BY ORB

FILLMORE WEST 6·7·8·9 MAY

© BILL GRAHAM 1971 · # 279   TEA LAUTREC LITHO · SAN FRANCISCO
ALL MACY'S TICKET OUTLETS · · · SAN FRANCISCO · FOX PLAZA BOX OFFICE NINTH & MARKET · CITY LIGHTS BOOKSTORE 261 COLUMBUS AVE. · THE TOWN SQUIRE,
1318 POLK · OUTSIDE IN 2544 MISSION   BERKELEY · DISCOUNT RECORDS · SHAKESPEARE, & CO.   SAUSALITO · THE TIDES   REDWOOD CITY · REDWOOD HOUSE
OF MUSIC   SAN MATEO · TOWN & COUNTRY RECORDS   SAN JOSE · DISCOUNT RECORDS   MENLO PARK · DISCOUNT RECORDS   SAN RAFAEL · RECORD KING
NEW OUTLETS : SAN FRANCISCO · MUSIC ODYSSEY 3628 GEARY   OAKLAND · SHERMAN·CLAY   HAYWARD · GENERAL STORE 24578 MISSION
SINGER

5

HIPPIE, INC.

Sometimes decades pass and nothing happens; and then sometimes weeks pass and decades happen.

—*Vladimir Lenin*

I F A GROUP of the original Haight-Ashbury hippie businesspeople had created a corporation that was called Hippie, inc.—committed to manufacturing, distributing, and selling products that were invented or reinvented or popularized by hippies during the first one hundred weeks of their movement, what would they still be selling today?

AUTHENTIC HIPPIE LABEL

The word "hippie" has become a catch-all label that is broadly applied to consumer products associated with the sixties counterculture, such as clothing (e.g., loose-fitting cotton apparel), music (e.g., folk/rock), ideas (e.g., eco-friendly), events (e.g., farmers markets), lifestyles (e.g., communal living), techniques (e.g., organic farming), diets (e.g., vegan) and dishes (e.g., tabouli). Therein lies the problem. Hippie is used to describe so many things that it has ended up accurately describing very little. For the purposes of this book, a product is defined as *authentically hippie* in its origin if it meets the following three criteria:

Possession: The product must be linked directly to authentic hippies, with evidence that the product was invented, reinvented, passionately endorsed or popularized by and in the possession of real hippies.

Location: The product must have been used by or in the possession of a hippie in or around the San Francisco Haight-Ashbury District or Santa Cruz.

Timing: The product must have been used by Haight-Ashbury hippies sometime between November 27, 1965 and October 6, 1967.

Employing these three guidelines, there are dozens of authentic hippie products that can be loosely grouped into Food and Drink, Clothing, Gear, and Other Hippie Styles (beliefs, books, music, home décor and the like). Some of these products were also part of the mainstream culture (corduroy clothing) or other subcultures (such as tattoos popular among bikers) and others were almost exclusive to the hippies (tie-dyed t-shirts, love beads).

HOW HAVE THEY FARED?

Businesspeople, especially marketers, would organize the list of hippie products into three broad categories, 1) product losers, 2) product stars, and 3) cash cows.

Product Losers

Ironically, many products and trends for which hippies are best known today are ones that fared the *worst*. Sitars, bongo drums, finger cymbals, white robes, costume-like shirts and dresses as well as the tendency toward wearing

Michael McClure, 1967

no shoes, bras, deodorant, or clothes were believed by many to be *typical* hippie products and trends. Given the demise of these items, some logically conclude that all hippie-originated or recreated products and trends ultimately failed, but they are mistakenly only looking at the product losers, which can be summed up as things that were some combination of difficult to obtain, unacceptable in public, uncomfortable and un-fun. This includes unusual musical instruments, costume-like garb, socially unacceptable outfits/behavior and impractical items like geodesic domes, animal hides, and hearses.

The losers meet at least one of these four criteria:

1. **They were/are nowhere to be found.** This group consists primarily of clothing items that never appeared in mainstream American retail stores even for a short time. Examples: transparent dresses, burlap skirts, animal robes, Mexican shirts worn as dresses, and George Washington frock coats.

2. **They were/are used primarily by "consumer outliers."** These include clothing and non-clothing items that are used by only a very few groups, such as survivalists, religious fanatics, hippie wannabes, and assorted others. Examples: tepees, bongos,

geodesic homes, white robes, Buddhist robes, fifes, as well as an acceptance of body odor and barefootedness.

3. **Dead-on-Arrival.** These products either never made it or were popular only for a short time and only in a few select locations. Examples include: dried banana skin cigarettes, finger cymbals, converted hearses and shaman sticks.

4. **Costumes.** These product non-starters include clothing that the hippies used as costumes to draw attention to themselves at public events, *and to this day* continue to be used primarily as costumes. Examples: tiaras, Arabesque pants, broad-striped pants, Cowboy-and-Indian attire, and puffy-sleeved (or "pirate") shirts for men.

The theoretical owners of Hippie, inc., would have been wise to quickly dump these items from their inventory and focus instead on their most successful product stars.

Product Stars

Product stars are often a company's most profitable products, distinguished from cash cows (discussed later) because they are not persistently or dependably profitable. These stars constitute Hippie, inc.'s largest category of merchandise. Body paint, bubble hoops (to make giant soap bubbles,) love beads, hemp products, and incense are some of the myriad of product stars that were popular among the hippies during the heyday of Haight-Ashbury and have made money in the decades since. Some were sleeper stars that took awhile to catch on and some were cyclical like fishnet tops for women and leather shirts. Others were market-specific like hookahs and t-shirts with images of Ché Guevara. The focus of this book, however, is not the product stars but the cash cows that have generated millions of dollars and in some cases, billions.

Product Cash Cows

Everybody loves a star, but for businesspeople, nothing sustains their companies over the long haul like cash cows. Usually the smallest of the three product groups, cash cows are highly profitable steady-Eddies. Cash cows include some of the best known brands in the world, such as Campbell's Chicken Noodle Soup, Ford pickup trucks, and Mars' Snickers ($3 billion-a-year candy bar). Cash cows are "milked" year after year, supplying a dependable flow of revenue. Were it to exist, Hippie, inc.'s, success would heavily rely on twenty-five cash cows. These cash cows (which include former product stars that ultimately became cash cows) came out of the hippie movement either as innovations (tie-dyed fabrics, folk/rock concerts) or popularizations (yoga, salad as a meal). They include:

* Army fatigues for civilian everyday wear
* breads, artisan and whole grain
* contemporary Christian worshiptainment
* exotic scents and oils (cedar, pathouli, jasmine, sandalwood, frankincense)

Selling the Oracle

* exotic spices and herbs
* folk/rock concerts
* granola type products
* interactive online social network communities
* jeans, faded/frayed
* marijuana
* men's non-traditional jewelry
* men's shoulder bags
* organic/health foods (stores, cafes, farmer's markets)
* posters, screen-printed and offset lithography
* psychedelic design motifs
* recycling
* rock/light shows
* salad as a meal
* solar/alternative energy
* tea with natural additives
* tie-dyed fabrics
* t-shirts, decorated with slogans
* vegetarian and/or vegan dishes and diets
* yoga and meditation
* yogurt and probiotic products

Some products, like microwave ovens, are immediate cash cows, but most take time, which explains why some of the hippie cash cows started off as sleepers. Yogurt and probiotics are examples of products that were sleepers for several decades before rising to stars with increased medical reports about their value, and finally to cash cows, with findings that indicate that some gastrointestinal problems can be satisfactorily solved with a simple daily dose of probiotics.

The products outlined here became part of the original hippie lifestyle, in their eating and drinking habits; their way of dressing, entertaining themselves and furnishing their living spaces; and in their sacred beliefs, practices and possessions. Understanding the core values of the Haight-Ashbury hippies and how those values were manifested in their daily lives, helps to identify those products and concepts that were associated with them as a consumer group. It stands to reason that a portion of the products that were in steady demand by the Haight-Ashbury community would be appealing to those outside it as well.

Hippie, inc., of course never existed. In 1965, hippies and the observers of their movement could only guess what products would enjoy enduring popularity over the next decades. Fifty years later, the guessing is over.

PART III

*

BASIC NEEDS

6

FOOD

I arrived in the Haight at age thirteen at the very beginning of the hippie movement . . . At first, I worked at the Good Earth commune located on Cole Street in the Panhandle. They made me a baker and three times a week I baked bread and cookies. The whole-grain food movement was just starting. The reason we got into whole wheat and natural foods was because we did not trust food manufacturers to provide healthy food. So Tsvi (Strauch), Hyla Deer, (Tsvi's wife) and the Diggers would make alternative food dishes—beans, rice, vegetarian dishes along with whole grains and sprouts, and lots of lentils. This was in 1966, and most Americans were eating steak—but not us.

—*Robert Limon*

THEIR LOCATION IN San Francisco, California, had a major impact on the hippies' food choices. The ethnically diverse city housed many different inexpensive ethnic restaurants and markets. The state has a twelve-month growing season and an enormous farm industry, so in 1965 plentiful fresh produce was on offer year round, and allowed the hippies to spark a reversal of food trends that had taken hold over the previous two decades.

Following the end of World War II consumption of fresh foods began plummeting across the country, including California. A major reason fresh food reached all-time lows in the 1960s was that during the post-war economic and technological boom, most American households acquired refrigerators with freezers. Though residential refrigerators with freezers were around in 1940, their widespread use was delayed by World War II. Improved freezing technology and a growing residential market spurred food manufacturers to offer an expanding variety of frozen and prepared foods to consumers. Time and again Americans opted for simpler and quicker ways to feed their families. They found the new, brightly packaged foodstuffs to be not just convenient but also glamorous in their modernity. Most middle-class Americans in 1965 were neither ready nor eager to spend the time and work necessary to prepare fresh meals when they could heat up TV dinners, frozen meat pies, and other frozen entrees prepared by companies like Swanson, Stouffers, Bird's Eye and Kraft Foods. Inevitably, by the 1960s demand for fresh produce and interest in cooking from scratch had dwindled.

Fresh and natural/organic foods were the foot soldiers in the war early hippies waged against the processed, pre-prepared, fatty, and salty foods most Americans were gobbling up in the 60s, two decades before medical researchers and nutritionists gave Americans reams of data showing the indisputable benefits of eating fresh fruits and vegetables and grains. If the hippies were the modern-day proselytizers of the idea of "eating fresh and natural," then the medical researchers from leading U.S. universities were the *opinion leaders* who provided the American food industry and consumers in the 1980s with ever-more compelling reasons to adjust their eating habits. The consumer response was astounding. U.S.D.A. data indicated that Americans ate an average of seventy pounds more commercially grown vegetables per capita and fifty-two pounds more fruit per capita in 1995 than in 1970.

The hippies' interest in fresh food did not only come from their appreciation of the virtues of healthy eating *per se*. Doubtless part of the impetus was the effect of repeated acid trips which, as suggested earlier, instilled a strong preference for the natural over the synthetic. Another, perhaps more powerful reason, hippies preferred fresh and natural was born of their desire to go "back to the earth"; to return to an earlier, simpler time when Americans sustained themselves with their own small farms and orchards, before multi-national food conglomerates dominated agriculture and before a profit-motivated industry focused on developing new technologies to sell higher-priced packaged foods to make Americans' lives easier.

The original hippies used:

* ingredients that were uncommon in the U.S. at the time, like bean sprouts and Indian herbs and spices
* main courses from foreign cuisines, such as paella
* grain-based dishes cooked with brown rice or bulgur wheat
* ethnic side dishes, like quesadillas
* a few dishes that were eccentric in 1966 and remain so to this day, like fried bananas and plantains
* uncommon product combinations, such as tea with organic honey
* items and eating practices that have, over time, become middle-class American staples (e.g., salad as a meal)

Dishes that were once thought exotic and hippie-ish—Indian samosas and pakoras dipped in chutneys and spiced yogurt, Thai curries ladled over steaming plates of Lebanese couscous and Greek pilaf have become part of the American diet, helping to push fruit and vegetable consumption to highs not seen for decades. One early hippie product, in particular, increased demand for oats, dried fruits, and nuts. Unusual at the time, granola today has turned into a billion-dollar consumer product—a staple of the American breakfast and, in the form of cereal bars, the American morning snack and coffee break. In 2009, granola products constituted a $1.7 billion industry. Granola didn't originate in the Haight but it was the hippies who popularized muesli and granola in the U.S.

Better transportation, better food technology, medical research, and the hippies have all contributed to the change in the American diet since the 60s. Drawing on Rachel Carson's environmentalism, Emerson's utopianism, vegetarian philosophy, and the teachings of holy men like Jesus and Buddha, the hippies planted the seeds that would eventually grow into a movement, inspiring Americans to "get back to the garden," and to throw in a few herbs and spices from other cultures to make the peas and carrots more palatable.

Now that millions of mainstream Americans eat more fresh fruit and veg-etables, buy organic food and shop at natural food stores, it is easy to forget that for the hippies the organic food movement was also a spiritual quest. At the board meeting of the Organic Merchants on Mount Shasta in 1970 with traces of snow still on the ground, eight thousand feet up, the merchants met "to plot a spiritual revolution based on ecological principles and food grown without pesticides, chemical sprays or fertilizers". After moments of silence in "gratitude for each other's presence" and "the lovely mountain" and "this beauti-ful planet of ours," after prayers and yoga postures, Fred Rohe, the founder and leader of the Organic Merchants led the assembled merchants in chants of "om." Om, Hindus believe, was the first sound vibration when life began. It was also the initials of the Organic Merchants. After the chanting Fred asked these 60 merchants why "they are here." They answered:

"We're here for love."

"We're a guiding light to distribute pure food."

"Our goal is to become God and to serve him."

"Our purpose is to serve the planet."

"We're here not only for the environment but for the world."

It is unlikely that these meditations, chants and spiritual musings are still uttered at the Whole Foods and Trader Joe's board meetings, but it shouldn't be forgotten how it all began.

The Organic Merchants combined their spiritual philosophies with prac-tical business ideas. In their stores besides selling wholesome food they gave out free handouts like The Sugar Story, The Oil Story, The NOT List (No Organic Truth) educating the public about the food industry. Some of these handouts were then reprinted in Underground Newspapers, enlarging the readership and customer base.

ETHNIC FOODS

Eating non-European ethnic cuisine (except for dining at Chinese and Mexi-can restaurants) was also rare until the hippies came along. The hippies placed a high premium on foreign products and ideas from the Middle East, Asia, the Indian subcontinent, Africa, and the Mediterranean. They ate ethnic food for both practical and ideological reasons. Convenience and cost played a part. However, sometimes the hippies' food choices were motivated by spiritual beliefs. For example, rice, tea, and vegetarian dishes had been staples of India for centuries. Many hippies held India in high regard. "India was our mother," former street kid Robert Limon explained. "The meditation, the music, the food, and the vegetarianism—the Indians could live on the cheap and live communally and that was what we wanted for ourselves."

Their enthusiasm for variety in their daily menu eventually caught on, ultimately, combined with increased non-European immigration, creating a billion-dollar ethnic food industry that today includes recipes, restaurants, and packaged foods.

TEA

(For us,) tea represented Zen, the Bhagavad Gita, and health.
—*Robert Limon*

(We talked) over tea and organic honey in his
Hashberry house one day.
—*Burton Wolfe*, **The Hippies**

Tea in China had been a common drink since the third century B.C. and popular in America for over 200 years before the hippies came along to revitalize it, mixing in natural additives such as honey, ginger, orange and marijuana. They followed the same path of continuous innovation as they did elsewhere and took an existing product and tweaked it with a new ingredient. Tea *in combination with a natural sweetener* is a prime example of a hippie product that in the decades since Haight-Ashbury's became a popular product star and is now a cash cow. Today Americans see nothing unusual about stirring honey, stevia, or agave into their tea either at home or in a cafe. But in the mid-1960s, most Americans wanting to sweeten their Lipton black tea used processed white sugar (in other countries and some parts of rural America honey and jam were used to sweeten tea before the hippies came along but it was the hippies who experimented with the combinations and spread the word). There once was a time when adding organic honey to tea was not just rare, but also a political statement, an act of defiance against sugar growers and manufacturers who, hoping to sweeten their own bottom line, turned perfectly natural raw sugar into unhealthy, processed white sugar. Both Burton Wolfe and Toni Del Renzio, who observed the original Haight-Asbury hippies, mentioned in their books seeing hippies drink tea with organic honey. Wolfe expounded on the "politics of honey" in an interview. "The philosophy adopted by the hippies was wrapped to a certain extent around the desire to return more to nature and away from what they called 'plastic.' Among the substances considered unnatural and unhealthful was sugar. Honey is made by bees; ergo it is natural—i.e., good."

Today, this old hippie ideal—using nature's own to make life qualitatively better—is embraced by millions of mainstream tea drinkers. In fact, the idea of tea in combination with something naturally sweet and something healthy practically defines the entire ready-to-drink (RTD) bottled tea market—a billion-dollar industry with brands like Arizona, Snapple and Peace Tea.

Within a short six years after the hippies began drinking and popularizing tea with organic honey, the Snapple Beverage Corporation and Celestial Teas were born. Snapple is today's leading American maker of single-serving iced tea drinks.

RTD tea is one part of the overall tea market in the U.S. with ties to the early hippies; herbal tea is another. Celestial Seasonings began in Colorado in 1969 when hippie disciples Mo Siegel, John Hay, and Peggy Clute started collecting wild herbs and flowers and selling them to health food stores in Boulder, Colorado. In 1984, after dramatic growth, Celestial Seasonings was bought by Kraft Foods. Today it is a part of the Hain Celestial Group and still going strong.

Overall, today's tea market is thriving. U.S. trade statistics report 519 million pounds of tea imports per year. In 2009, industry revenue for tea products was $2.1 billion.

Nancy Van Brasch Hamren—Yogurt and Probiotics

Nancy Van Brasch Hamren, who in conjunction with Chuck and Sue Kesey, owners of Springfield Creamery, spearheaded the modern-day yogurt and probiotic industries and are credited with being the first creamery to culture probiotic strains in yogurt. Nancy learned to appreciate yogurt from her health-conscious grandmother, who was part of a health-food movement in the Bay Area in the 1940's. Nancy graduated from high school in Pasadena, CA, moved to San Francisco 1966 and worked as a bank teller while attending San Francisco State University. She lived in the Haight with her boyfriend. "It was a wonderful, exciting time," she writes on her website. "The civil rights movement and Vietnam protests, and free speech movements were happening, and a big part of this consciousness-raising was a discussion of natural foods." In the summer of 1969 she and her boyfriend took care of Ken Kesey's Oregon farm while he was in London, making a recording of stories with the Beatles. When summer ended, Nancy, looking for a job, visited Chuck Kesey's (Ken's brother and fellow Prankster) Springfield Creamery. She was hired as a bookkeeper, and together with Chuck, worked on perfecting her yogurt recipe. The Springfield Creamery today has a fully cultured product line of Nancy's yogurt, Nancy's cottage cheese, Nancy's Kefir, Nancy's Soy Yogurt, and other products that are mainstays in many homes. Jerry Garcia and the Grateful Dead gave a benefit concert in Oregon in1972 to help the struggling creamery and Huey Lewis before he became famous was a partner in a company that trucked Nancy's Yogurt to San Francisco.

Up until the time of the hippies, yogurt in America was mostly consumed by members of Middle Eastern and some European-American immigrant communities, thanks to immigrant-started companies like Dannon, who brought yogurt over from the old country. Around 1969, that all began to change. Nancy's and Chuck's interest was not only in yogurt but the health-giving probiotic component of authentically cultured yogurt products. Probiotics—in yogurt and now in pill form—became popular with the introduction of probiotic brands, like Activia and Align, in the late-1990s, and today, millions of Americans include probiotics in their daily regimen.

What is Nancy's and the Kesey family's Springfield Creamery contribution to Hippie, inc.? The burgeoning yogurt and probiotic industry they helped initiate in the U.S.A. was worth over $7 billion in 2015.

The Digger Women—Artisan Breads

When we first started, we baked the bread in the basement of the All Saints Church. We would knead the dough and put it into cans and bake it. We would give loaves away at the Free Frame of Reference (located at the time at the corner of Cole and Carl streets.) It was kind of like a fair. There were also some people who had bees and were selling local honey and we would spread this on our baked bread. Whole wheat once was used to bake bread, but no longer. (In the mid-sixties) it was white bread that Americans wanted to eat—mass-produced in plastic bags. At the time, manufacturers made bread with processed white flour. To preserve it longer, they would add ingredients that were really unnecessary—chemicals and preservatives—otherwise it would mold quickly. I really think that the legacy of the Digger Bread is that it brought whole wheat back and shunned white bread. But you know, for us, it was just a lot of fun—we would knead dough all day, strip off our clothes, and go swimming (laughter).

—*Jane Lapiner*

The Haight-Ashbury Diggers believed that America was rich enough to help those in need and provided free food as well as medical care and temporary housing. A small group of hard-working women made the Diggers' most enduring contribution to the quality of life in America. These women were pioneers of the modern-day artisan and whole grain breads industry. There were seven in particular: Paula, Phyllis, Jane Lapiner, Cindy Small, Bobsie, Nina Blasenheim, and Natural Suzan. The Digger women baked crusty, wholesome bread together to feed the hungry—the first documented distribution of whole-grain artisan bread in post-WWII America. Ingredients for the bread were mostly donated. ("Free bread" is a misnomer—obviously someone had to pay to grow, harvest, and produce the necessary grains. It was rumored that Emmett Grogan—who had a history of petty thievery in Brooklyn, NY, before moving to the Haight—stole items to help the cause.) These women, along with other Diggers, reintroduced a type of bread and a style of baking that had fallen out of favor with most American homemakers by 1966. Before the hippies Wonder Bread and its white flour counterparts ruled the ovens. The Digger women's efforts helped influence American consumers' bread tastes, which ultimately led to the creation of a billion-dollar artisan bread industry. In 2013, Jane Lapiner was honored by famed American chef and restaurant owner Alice Waters for her pioneering work with whole-grain artisanal breads during the time that she was a Digger.

While the Diggers advocated giving away products to those in need, not all of the original hippies were so inclined. In fact, contrary to popular opinion, a number of hippies were good businessmen, including our next Hippie, inc., shareholder.

Fred Rohe—Natural Food Stores

Transforming the traditional health food store model into a new style of operation was the previously mentioned founder of the Organic Merchants, Fred Rohe. Originally from White Plains, New York, he grew up interested in literature and sports. Rebellious, he spent more time in school detention than doing homework. Fred left New York in 1959, inspired by the Jack Kerouac novel *On The Road*, joining the beat movement in San Francisco's North Beach and the hippie movement as it developed in the 60s.

His business ideas were inspired by shopping at Thom's Health Foods in the Richmond district of San Francisco. Thom's combined elements of the traditional health store with an emphasis on body building supplements. Fred was intrigued, but his ideas about what a natural food store should be diverged from what he saw at Thom's. The fundamental difference was that he thought a better approach would be to focus on traditional whole foods, rather than supplements and specialty items. And the name—natural foods rather than health foods—would reflect the changed emphasis. His most important inspiration was photos he saw of interiors of early twentieth century grocery stores.

So, in April of 1965 he bought Sunset Health Foods (at 1319 Ninth St. in the Sunset district, neighboring the Haight-Ashbury), which had been a traditional health store. Here, Fred worked on his ideas until the store morphed into New Age Natural Foods; it was to become the prototype for the modern-day natural foods store—places like Whole Foods Market and Trader Joes's.

> By 1970, we had grown so much that we moved to a second location, in Palo Alto, where we operated out of a 10,000 square foot defunct supermarket. The Palo Alto store was the first "all-under-one-roof" natural foods store. It was so big, I remember having to make six facings (rows) instead of two just to make it look like we were fully stocked (laughter). The store had a butcher shop, so I took it out and replaced it with a vegetarian delicatessen that served salads, sandwiches, and so forth. This might have been my own idea, or someone else may have already invented the vegetarian deli by then—I don't know for sure. But I think there was one thing we pioneered—the gravity-fed bulk bins for things like grains, beans, and seeds that customers opened to fill their bags.

> —Fred Rohe

Tsvi Strauch described Rohe as a "hippie-yogi type, whose place was extremely popular with the hippies." Easily one of the most prolific hippie entrepreneurs to emerge during the Haight-Ashbury movement, Fred Rohe, founded America's:

* **first natural foods supermarket** (New Age Natural Foods)
* **first natural foods café** (The Good Karma Café)
* **first natural foods wholesale company and distribution center** (New Age Distributing Company)
* **first natural foods trade association** (Organic Merchants, OM)

Interest in natural food stores started growing in about 1967 and has continued for five decades. Over the years adopters have joined the hippie bandwagon and the two largest natural foods stores in the U.S. are Whole Foods Market and Trader Joe's. By 2015, the two chains combined had over 800 stores and approximately $25 billion in sales.

In the decades following the hippie movement, Fred Rohe has continued working on and off in the natural products industry, also writing several books including the *Complete Book of Natural Foods, Nature's Kitchen, The Zen of Running,* and *Dr. Kelley's Answer to Cancer.* He is also one of the founders of the Natural Health Yellow Pages. His most recent work is the combination book/website, *The Smart Food Movement: Organic for Real.*

A teen rebel (Fred), a former bank teller (Nancy), and a big hearted college student (Jane), teamed up with the Organic Merchants, the Kesey family, and Jane's Digger sisters. Together they led the way creating thousands of jobs, billions of dollars in revenue, and changing the landscape of what Americans eat.

PRESENTED IN SAN FRANCISCO   BY BILL GRAHAM

TIM BUCKLEY

COUNTRY JOE & THE FISH — primal HEAD LIGHTS Stimulation

© 1967 Bill Graham No 59

FILLMORE AUD

FRI · SAT · APR 14-15   8PM $1   SUN APR 16   2PM TO 7PM
                          2AM $3½

Pete Bailey

TICKETS SAN FRANCISCO: City Lights Bookstore; S.F. State College (Hut T-1); The Town Squire (1318 Polk); Kelley Galleries (3681A Sacramento);
Wild Colors (1418 Haight); Bally Lo (Union Square); BERKELEY: Discount Records; Shakespeare & Co.; SAN MATEO: Town & Country Records;
REDWOOD CITY: Redwood House of Music; PALO ALTO: Dana Morgan Music; SAN RAFAEL: Record King; SAUSALITO: The Tides Bookstore

7

CLOTHING

Hippies forever changed the way fashion functions.

—*Lauren D. Whitley,* curator in the David and Roberta Logie Department of Textile and Fashion Arts at the Museum of Fine Arts, Boston, **Hippie Chic,** 2013

The Hippie cult itself, with its beads and drugs and outlandish clothes, may soon flower and die. But it will not leave our civilization unchanged.

—*Joseph Thorndike,* **Horizon Magazine,** 1968

The British Mod style, called mod gear, preceded the hippie style and Peggy Caserta played an important role. Peggy later was one of Janis' (Joplin) lovers and she had a shop down the street from our place, called Mnasidika. When we all first opened, Peggy sold "Mod" clothes and then, eventually, she moved over to hippie styles. The mod style was British and it started here at the Town Squire on Polk street in San Francisco. Then Lenard Nathan went to London buying British bobby capes and selling them at his UFO gallery in the Haight-Ashbury.

—*Tsvi Strauch*

POPULAR WISDOM TELLS us that the hippies cared little about appearances. Indeed, the hippies prided themselves on a lack of self-consciousness and refusal to conform to society's expectations. Haight-Ashbury's original hippies viewed conventional and gender-dictated styles

and grooming practices as masks that hid the true inner person. Their rock stars served as role models and were happy to parade this new approach to clothing and gear on the public stage, from the elaborate costumed look to the uniform of grungy tattered jeans and tangled hair to—when the time seemed right—going naked.

Nevertheless, it is oversimplification to suggest that the hippies didn't care at all about fashion. Tsvi Strauch explained that there was no single hippie style of clothing, but rather there were six distinct styles. The first style is what we refer to in this book as the "no" approach, which was very pedestrian— torn jeans, cotton tent dresses, and t-shirts. This look was adopted by The Grateful Dead, Big Brother and the Holding Company, and another band, called The Mystery Trend. The second look was the mod look, which origi- nated in England and included skinny pants, Beatle boots, and shag haircuts. This look was exemplified by the early Beatles, the Rolling Stones, the War- locks, before Jerry made them into The Grateful Dead, and Bob Dylan shortly after he moved from acoustic to electric guitar. The third look was the Western look, which consisted of cowboy hats and boots with fringed vests. Buffalo Springfield, which included Stephen Stills and Neil Young, wore this style. So did the Charlatans. The fourth was the Native American/Ethnic look, which included clothing embellished with beads, feathers, and embroidery. In Gear, the shop owned by Tsvi and Hyla Strauch, catered to this customer and look, and it was exemplified by Janis Joplin, who was a steady customer, buying her love beads and the Russian fur hat she frequently wore. The fifth was the Retro/Vintage look that took its cue from Victorian and Edwardian fashion—long frilly skirts, high necks, chokers, and the like. The Charlatans also wore this style as did a poster artist by the name of Terré. This style didn't last at all but it did come back for a short while with mainstream Americans in the 1970s. Lastly, a sixth look, the handmade high quality cus- tom designed clothes that designers like Jeanne Rose, Linda Gravenites and Judy Dugan created.

With the hippies there were always contradictions and irony. The sub- culture that didn't care about money ended up generating great wealth; the slovenly, poorly dressed, tattered bohemians became a major influence in high

John Hendricks (member, ph phactor band)

Jeanne Rose and Janis Joplin in center modeling Jeanne Rose designs

fashion and also created fashion styles that changed the way mainstream Americans dressed. And as eager as some hippies were to reject mainstream ways and fashions, many readily embraced their own counter-conventions. When it came to what to wear each day, these hippies displayed a surprising conformity. The hippies' aversion to society's pretensions led them, ironically, to develop their version of what constituted acceptable attire. "We had a dress code—long hair to your shoulders, army jacket, and Levi jeans," Robert Limon recalls. "This is what you wore if you were a real hippie."

PRODUCT STARS THAT BECAME CASH COWS

The term "personal gear" means products people use to help accomplish their everyday tasks and that includes clothing, fashion accessories and other functional items. Collectively, personal gear and clothing styles make up what marketers call a product constellation that distinguishes one group of consumers from another. Yuppies might favor Rolex watches, BMWs, and Gucci briefcases while Crunchies might wear Birkenstocks, drive a Prius, and shop at the local food co-op. Personal gear and clothing styles help marketers create consumer profiles, which businesspeople use to anticipate and meet customer needs and wants.

Many of the products from the hippie "product constellation" came and went as fashion statements in the 60s, while others come and go cyclically. But some products have consistently sold well through the decades. Hippie personal gear and fashions that appeared in the sixties and continue to be used today have had a long time to generate wealth and contribute to the success of producers, retailers, and marketers. Four products that star in both eras are frayed/faded jeans, graphic tee-shirts and tie-dyed clothing, military surplus and camouflage clothing, and men's shoulder bags and non-traditional jewelry.

Jefferson Airplane with Signe Anderson

Blue Cheer

Frayed Jeans

> In 1964, the boys in Sacramento Valley where I lived just before I
> moved to the Haight in 1965 would buy brand new jeans and never
> wash them because they didn't want to ruin the creases and fade the
> colors. They wanted their jeans to look like they were just bought, all
> nicely creased and deep blue. Within months, that all changed.
>
> —*Penelope de Vries*

In the yearly bounty of fresh fashions designed and retailed for America's young consumers over the last five decades, one item has managed to prevail more or less unchanged—faded blue jeans. In his book on the early hippies Del Renzio recounts the story of a dancing hippie named Tumbleweed wearing "deliberately frayed jeans" during an impromptu gathering of a Haight-Ashbury hippie tribe. Hippies turned the beat-up, tattered, well-worn look of old blue jeans into a cutting-edge fashion statement. Deliberately frayed fabric now has an industry name: distressed denim.

Plain old denim dungarees were around long before the distressed look, originating in Italy some four hundred years ago. The uniform of the day laborer, in the last half of the twentieth century in the U.S. jeans frequently symbolized youthful revolt. Fifties rebels James Dean and Elvis Presley wore jeans, although neither wore jeans that were frayed—deliberately or accidentally—in public or on screen. The hippies were some of the first people to do that.

Haight-Ashbury hippies were strong idealists and two of their most dearly held ideals were the American principles of democracy and equality. Although many in the mainstream saw hippies as subversive (and, to be sure, some were), hippies tended to see themselves as the real American patriots, purists who upheld the true spirit of the U.S. Constitution. Many hippies manifested their populist convictions by identifying with "the common man." In particular, the hippies had a strong empathy for the blue-collar worker and the working poor, believing that American corporations and the government exploited the labor of the masses to enrich the few. And nothing quite symbolized the working man's plight in the mid-1960s better than tattered work pants.

Today, the association that distressed denim once had with the hardscrabble lives of America's workers has all but disappeared. Faded jeans have become solidly middle-class. At the 2010 Winter Olympics, the tattered-looking jeans were the official dress of the U.S. snowboarding team, who proudly displayed these symbols of American youthful rebellion and national pride before a worldwide audience.

Tie-dyed Clothing and Graphic T-shirts

Judith organized a free sewing shop and tie-dye center. In there, women were taught how to tie the knots and use the dyes, and people would come in off the street all day long to have the clothes they were wearing mended, or made more interesting with colorful tie-dye patterns and sewn-on patches. Soon, their tie-dyed clothing was seen everywhere in the district and a handful of girls who learned the basics from Judith and the others went to work for the HIP shops, massproducing tie-dyed items into a fashion that eventually spread throughout the country.

—*Emmett Grogan,* **Ringolevio: A Life Played for Keeps**

Two remarkable women originated hippie tie-dyed clothing and fabrics: Judith Godlhaft and Luna Moth Robbin (a.k.a. Jodi Robbin and Jodi Paladini). Judith was a Cornell graduate born into a family of socialist activists. Luna Moth Robbin, an artist who worked in numerous media including textiles, was the woman who popularized the art of tie-dyeing that became synonymous with the idea of "hippies." Tie-dye was introduced in order to change mass-produced white shirts into unique hand crafted creations. It's ironic that those efforts stirred a fashion trend that became one of the most recognized accoutrements of the Haight-Ashbury hippies, and ultimately created a billion-dollar mass produced product.

Goldhaft explained how the tie-dye craze came into being:

Judith Goldhaft tie-dying

The Free Store received many men's white shirts—the uniform that men in the 1950s and 60s wore going to work—that were being discarded. Karl Rosenberg, a painter, brought over a fabric artist named Jodi Robbin to consider what to do with the shirts and she suggested that they could be transformed from their mass industrial conformity by individuals tie-dying them. Each person would have a one-of-a-kind item that he or she had produced.

The first tie-dye workshop took place in the basement of a church on Waller Street. Many more tie-die workshops were held, some in the Free Stores, but many other places as well. Luna initially instructed us, Nina, Phyllis, other Diggers, and me. We then all taught lots of other people to tie-dye. I also assisted Luna at some of her more formal teaching sessions at colleges and community centers.

The art of tie-dye, a technique called Shibori in Japan, originated some six thousand years before the hippies started folding, scrunching, twisting, and dunking white t-shirts into tubs of dye. Once the hippies started, the economic impact was quick and astounding. Tsvi Strauch remembers:

> Hyla and I sold some of this stuff in our shop but most of it really took off when it was sold at the Dead concerts. All the selling was in the parking lot and some of those kids made $100,000 a year just selling tie-dye shirts in the parking lot of the Dead concerts."

Besides tie-dye t-shirts, graphic t-shirts also became hugely popular during the sixties. With symbols of revolt like marijuana and Cesar Chavez printed on the shirts, Mouse and Warren Dayton were two of the pioneers, growing a world wide industry that continues to thrive and generate billions of dollars decade after decade.

However, for Diggers like Judy and Luna it was never about the money. They were interested in social interactions and the betterment of lives and society. Judy says that it is difficult now for people to "understand the lack of greed and consumerism that existed" during that period. A memoriam for Luna Moth Robbin states that she "always found ways to inject light and design into community activism." For example, in the 70s, she designed a silkscreen of the endangered Mission Blue Butterfly and helped make t-shirts and banners at celebrations to support the Committee to Save San Bruno Mountain. In the 80s and 90s she worked with community groups and children in Hawaii using art to educate about the environment.

Today Judith Goldhaft runs the 501(c)(3) ecological educational nonprofit Planet Drum Foundation, which was founded by her life-partner Peter Berg.

Military Fatigues

We were the army of peace—that's why we wore the Army jacket.

—*Robert Limon*

Haight-Ashbury hippies donned Army-surplus military attire in 1966, sparking a fashion trend among American youth that continued unabated until the end of the Vietnam War in 1975. After that, the trend took a short breather and shirked its anti-war symbolism before charging ahead into what has be-

Marty Balin

come today a bonanza for makers and sellers of camouflage and olive drab clothing (note: camouflage had been used by non-hippie artists in France long before the Hippie Movement and by beats in the U.S. in the 1950s).

In the mid-1960s, Haight-Ashbury hippies actually constituted a small proportion of the U.S. civilian population who wore Army fatigues. A larger group consisting of hunters and outdoorsmen purchased them at Army surplus stores. Army surplus stores have always been plentiful in cities like San

Francisco that housed military bases, and in the 1960s, the city was home to two posts: the Presidio and the Alameda Naval Air Station at Alameda.

The early hippies regarded wearing fatigues as a way of identifying with the foot soldier and the revolutionary mercenary fighting on behalf of the people. Still, the hippies had practical reasons for wearing military clothes: fatigues were readily available, cheap to buy, very durable, and appropriate for their own outdoor lives in the cool San Francisco climate. The distinction that the hippies have over hunters and outdoorsmen and the beats is that they popularized wearing military fatigues not simply for recreation but as everyday clothing. By the simple technique of changing the use of an existing product and then exploiting the world-wide media attention given to the hippies, camouflage clothing morphed into a cash cow.

Men's Shoulder Bags and Non-Traditional Jewelry

It was Herb Caen, the journalist from the *Chronicle*, who coined the term "love beads." We were one of the first sellers of love beads in the Haight and before Herb, we called them Mojo or Ju-Ju, like: 'I'm going to wear my Mojo or Ju-Ju." Herb wrote a column for the *Chronicle* in which he told readers to go to the Haight and buy their "love beads." So the name stuck after that and Mojo and Ju-Ju were lost to time.

—*Tvsi Strauch*

Two additional examples where the hippies transformed the use of an existing accessory were men's shoulder bags and non-traditional jewelry. Men in other cultures carried bags, native men wore jewelry, and there were dandies in France and England and even a few in the United States in the 1800s who wore stickpins and other non-traditional jewelry, but until the hippies these were not acceptable or widespread fashion items for men.

In the United States there is still a stigma associated with men carrying "purses." Nevertheless, it would be a mistake to dismiss men's bags as an insignificant market appealing only to a small group. From computer bags to duffel bags to satchels to messenger bags– the industry for men's bags is substantial. This wasn't always the case. Early hippie merchant Tvsi Strauch remembers:

> Before the mid-1960s, a man would not be caught dead using a bag—
> even when he was, in fact, *using a bag*. For example, a man carrying a
> satchel or duffel bag would be real reluctant to use the shoulder strap
> but rather, he would tuck it, awkwardly and uncomfortably, up under
> his arm. You'd even see this with men and their briefcases. There
> was just something about a bag or case swinging freely from a man's
> clutched fist that was too feminine for most American men in the fifties.

Tsvi and his wife Hyla's ideas for a man's shoulder bag were influenced by three places: Berkeley, Cambridge and Sierra Madre in Mexico. First, in 1952 when Strauch was attending Berkeley, he noticed that the only men who had bags were American esthetes, European students, and American vets who used

green duffle bags with a drawstring. One of Tsvi's professors, Alain Renoir—a Harvard graduate and son of the film director Jean Renoir and grandson of the artist Pierre-Auguste Renoir—was always carrying a funny little bag that he would fling over his shoulder. In 1959, when Strauch took up his graduate work at Harvard, he saw a similar green bag that was used at the time only by Harvard men. Ever the entrepreneur, he tucked away these chance "bag encounters" until a few years later:

> I had my first acid trip in 1964 and I started wearing more jewelry after that, particularly Native American jewelry. Hyla and I took a trip to Mexico in 1965 and met up with the Huichol Indians. The Huichol use peyote as a religious sacrament and the men wore highly-embroidered bags. When Hyla and I got back to the US in 1965, I started to carry a bag like that at our gallery B'tzalel in Pacific Heights.

> Within a year they were also stocking jewelry for men.

> Before we got into the business men wore only two kinds of jewelry: watches and wedding bands. After we got into it, the product line quickly expanded to include bracelets and necklaces. But not just any bracelet and necklace—we're talking large chains with peace signs and crosses hanging from them. Women wore these too, and our merchandise represented some of the first moves toward 'uni-sex fashions.'

Tsvi's journey to becoming a hippie merchant and trendsetter began in Vienna where he was born soon after the Nazis invaded in 1938. His parents escaped to Belgium and when Tsvi was three years old they emigrated to the United States, settling in San Francisco. An avid reader of ancient history, Tsvi didn't mind when he was sent to the cloak room as a punishment in school for acting up. The room had shelves filled with history books.

When his mother, like many Jewish boys' moms, didn't allow him to play tackle football, he went out for the cross country team. The team won the San Francisco championship twice and in his senior year he also placed third in the city pole vault championship. It was in high school where he started to find his voice, hearing a teacher make racist remarks about blacks, he stood up and reprimanded her to the applause of his classmates.

Tsvi and Hyla (grandniece of Leon Trotsky) came early to the party in the Haight and stayed late. In 2014, Tsvi was still running a shop in The Lower Haight called Gallery 683 that offered tribal art (textiles, drums, masks, jewelry, and other artifacts) "from the Americas and beyond."

By 2015, the two industries Hyla and Tsvi helped originate in the mid-sixties (men's shoulder bags and men's non-traditional jewelry) were worth over a billion dollars combined.

LEGACY

The hippies changed high fashion and low fashion. They popularized distressed jeans, shoulder bags and jewelry for men, screen printed t-shirts, military fatigues and tie-died clothes. They set forth a vibrant array of colors and styles in new combinations that freed fashion designers to transcend conventions. Lauren Whitley says, in her book, *Hippie Chic*, that the "Hippies, swathed in trippy colors, retro fabrics, fur, and fringe, made clothing a canvas of personal expression, forever changing how we relate to what we wear." She goes on to say that "For the first time, high-end designers weren't dictating all the trends. Instead, many new styles originated on the streets, with the other revolutions, and trickled upward through hip boutiques into the top fashion houses."

The hippies also paved the way for future subcultures to impact the mainstream—their ideas and products springing from the street. Hip-hop clothing and style is a good example of this dynamic today, where visual stimuli—blogs, media attention, ads with celebrities—can push street garb from local-wear-only to international fashion trends. Instantaneous world-wide media permits simultaneous diffusion; whereas, in the hippie era, trends were powered through the less pervasive media of three-channel television, magazines, newspapers, and radio. But the mechanism of a subculture marketing and packaging themselves is the same (whether intentional or by chance,) utilizing the media to translate the energy in the street into a trend and finding opinion leaders, regardless of whether they are college newspaper editors or rap stars, to help deliver the message.

The Grateful Dead in Front of Peggy Caserta's shop, Mnasidika

When the hippies started their fashion revolution they also grandfathered hip-hop, grunge and punk fashions because they didn't merely create a new style of clothes—they created a new way of doing business and changed the dynamics of an industry. The adult world that the hippies rebelled against on so many levels was certainly not going to tell them what to wear. The hippies created a real revolution—they transferred power to the young.

8

SHELTER

I N THE BASIC needs of food and clothing, the hippies helped change the way we eat and dress. Besides leveraging their media clout and popularizing a slew of products and ideas, they produced innovators like Nancy Hamren, Fred Rohe, Judith Goldhaft, Luna Moth Robbin and Mouse, spearheading new product lines and new industries. To a lesser extent, hippies influenced shelter but it's still worth mentioning because the patterns of influence are similar to the other basic needs. Given the hippies track record of changes to the mainstream culture, it feels legitimate to point out the hippies' prescience and give them some credit for being at the forefront of several successful home products and ideas.

SHABBY CHIC

Having dropped out of mainstream society and turned their backs on conventional expectations, the original hippies sought to conduct their daily lives in ways that stayed true to their core values. This meant designing their living spaces to be simple, warm, and welcoming.

The hippies felt compelled to rebel against the direction mainstream American taste was headed. Consider John Steinbeck's description of a motel from *Travels with Charley*, a book about his 1960 journey across the country:

Everything was done in plastics—the floors, the curtains, table of stainless, burnless (sic.) plastic. Only the bedding and the towels were of natural material. I went to the small restaurant run in conjunction. It was all plastic too—the table linen, the butter dish. The sugar and crackers were wrapped in cellophane, the jelly in a small plastic coffin sealed in cellophane. Even the waitress wore a sponge-off apron.

In contrast, Burton Wolfe in *The Hippies* describes how some hippies lived in "crowded, musty, antiquated apartments and flats that they called "pads," often furnished with little more than a table and mattresses, and decorated with Oriental rugs, bamboo curtains, bells, and wine bottles." Tsvi Strauch elaborates: "The look the hippies wanted for their apartments stood in contrast to the modern artificial look at the time that was popular in the suburbs —the ranch-style home, ceramic tile, plastic knick-knacks, stainless steel appliances, Melmac dishes, vinyl siding, and wall-to-wall carpeting—these were totally out with the hippies. For them the suburban look reflected a cold culture interested in social standing and one-upmanship."

The question of who actually gave birth to the "shabby chic" style of home decorating may never be satisfactorily answered. Most agree that shabby chic first appeared in Britain, in the look of old country cottages with their tea-stained table cloths, worn chintz-covered sofas, and chipped window sills and door frames exposing decades' worth of paint layers. As far back as the seventeenth century, British aristocrats put a high value on patina (the beauty of an old, well-used surface, such as darkened leather on chairs or cracked-oil-paint finish on family portraits), which they felt distinguished their possessions from those of the upstart *nouveau riche*, whose things were too new, no matter how costly, to have acquired the look of centuries-old family treasures.

In modern-day America, the term "shabby chic" appeared in the 1980s in the pages of *World of Interiors* magazine. During the 1990s, furniture painters created a "shabby chic" look by rubbing and sanding off the top coats of oft-painted furniture to expose the original wood along with earlier base coats, which created an old, weathered look. So-called "faux painting" soon became an American middle-class arts-and-crafts hobby, and by the end of the 1990s (in part thanks to Peter Mayle's 1990 fabulously successful book, *A*

Rick Griffin

Year in Provence) the shabby look progressed from Mediterranean villas and West Coast beach houses to Middle American tract homes.

However, three decades before the shabby chic look peaked in popularity, North Beach beats and Haight-Ashbury hippies were decorating their homes in shabby ways that were quite chic. A point of origin may be traced back to 1955 in North Beach with the opening of a restaurant/cabaret/theater, called The Old Spaghetti Factory. Owner, Freddie Kuh, is described by Tsvi Strauch as a "gay, Jewish, artistic, hipster business owner who couldn't sit still and seemed to be everywhere." He filled his business with old and discarded junk—19th century torn-and-tattered chairs, carpets, and couches sat alongside wooden crates, medicine bottles, and stained glass on old, oiled wooden floors—which the artistic Kuh somehow managed to arrange in a manner that effused warmth and comfort.

Just as the hippies chose to wear deliberately torn and frayed jeans, in their homes they preferred the old and tattered over the shiny and new. Of course, like the land-rich but cash-poor English lords and ladies who found it convenient to put a high value on the old and worn, in part the cash-strapped hippies were making a virtue of necessity.

Two national business franchises whose merchandise was heavily influenced by this trend were Cost Plus Imports, which was founded on the San Francisco Wharf in 1958 and Pier 1 Imports, which was founded in 1962 in San Mateo, CA, opening for business in the Bay Area at the same time that first the beats and then the hippies were introducing this shabby chic style into the old, Victorian houses of North Beach and Haight-Ashbury. According to the company's web site, the original Pier 1 stores stocked love beads and incense in an effort to appeal to hippies and hippie wannabes. Today Pier 1 sells a variety of furniture accessories that are distinctively "hippie," including candles, vases, picture frames, cloth room dividers, woven baskets, denim-and leather-upholstered furniture, screen-printed posters, and wall decor, items often imported from India, China, and Latin America. While little of the original hippies' furnishings remain, the fundamental hippie style of the Haight represents a sizable portion of the Pier 1 inventory to this day. Their website still boasts the mantra "from hippie to hip." Pier 1 and Cost Plus World Market combined have over 500 stores and in 2013 had revenues over one billion dollars.

HIPPIE AESTHETIC

The comforting ambiance hippies sought was also achieved when they peeled back layers of "improvements" made by former occupants who had replaced or covered the original, natural materials used to construct their houses and apartments with manmade substitutes, such as plastic counter-tops and vinyl siding. The hippies were restoring old houses and reclaiming wooden floors while much of the rest of the country was binging on carpeting. Tvsi Strauch, who was running a business and helping raise a family in the Haight at the time, recalled how people would either move into low-cost rentals that had wooden floors, or they would tear up the carpet to expose the floors underneath:

> For the beats, the wood floors and high ceilings might have been
> mostly artsy because that was what they were all about. But for the

hippies it wasn't about art. A lot of hippies thought the world would end any day from nuclear war between Russia and the U.S. So a lot of them were withdrawing and returning to the comforts of home—waiting for the bomb to destroy everything. Because of this doomsday feeling, a lot of the hippies turned to their families and kids—they didn't want to go out and contribute to the 'war machine,' so instead they set up their cozy, warm homes with their spouses and kids and tried to make money any way they could without getting involved with the government and big business. Exposed wood projected the warm feeling that the hippies were looking for at the time.

The warmth of the hippie apartment was accented by accessories, many of which had long been available but unpopular with American decorators of the day. Candles, cotton drapes, lamps with stained-glass shades, floor pillows, beaded room dividers, tribal drums, pampas grass, woven baskets, conch shells, bamboo furniture, and richly colored carpets from Asia and the Middle East provided a lush, natural feel. Incense or joss sticks, massage oils, homemade soaps, and sachets of spice-stuffed cheesecloth bags lent the hippie pad the aroma of nature and the exotic. Patchouli, sandalwood, and jasmine replaced the intrusive chemical smells of the typical 1950s ranch home, such as ammonia, bleach, floor wax, furniture polish, glass cleaner, fabric softener, room aerosol, oven cleaner, spray deodorant, paint, and glue.

The hippies extended their distinctive decorating touch to the walls and shelves of their homes by using screen-printed and photo-offset posters and record album covers to adorn their rooms. Album covers, transformed by hippie artists into works of commercial art, now took on the added function of home decoration—at least for hippie pads.

SUMMARY

A major part of the hippie's ethos was going back to the natural, moving away from the plastic and synthetic world they perceived. This powerful core value manifested itself in changes to the basic human needs of shelter, food, and clothing. In shelter, the hippies were ahead of their time and influential, however, it was in food and clothing that the hippies contributed substantial enduring changes and their products created billions of dollars.

Had they stopped at the basics their legacy of cultural influence and wealth creation would still be enormous, but they wanted to create a new order, one that involved feeding the soul. From the beginning, part of their quest when they arrived in Haight-Ashbury, was a spiritual one.

PART IV

✳

FEEDING THE SOUL

9

EMBRACING
THE DIVINE

I was raised to be an object—the pretty girl. I was a homecoming queen, a cheerleader . . . And my mom's goal for me was to use my beauty to marry well. But after I left home, I just wanted nothing to do with that. I wanted something that would feed my soul. I didn't want to spend the rest of my life at the hair dresser and doing my nails . . .

—*Penny DeVries*

Traditional religions were not something the counter culture embraced. A lot of alternative religions were starting up. There was a fascination with the East, with Zen Budhism, Tibetian Budhism, India. There were a number of pioneers including Michael Murphy who started Esalen, Baba Ram Das—Richard Alpert—Leary's research partner at Harvard, Larry Brilliant, Wavy Gravy—Hugh Romney at the time, all went to India . . . and a lot of that was getting brought back here."

—*Eric Christensen*

"Eventually, all hippie creations, happenings, philosophies, minds, and bodies become channeled into one path. To the hippie that path leads to God and nirvana."

—*Burton H. Wolfe,* **The Hippies**

ALTHOUGH THE HIPPIES rejected the organized religions of their childhoods, with hide-bound rituals that no longer spoke to them, many of the concepts they chose to say "no" to—war, avarice, lying, phoniness, oppression of the poor—reflected values consistent with core teachings of every major religion. Things they chose to say "yes" to like yoga and meditation moored them to ancient religious practices. Not surprisingly, they satisfied their yearning for greater meaning in an eclectic way.

SPIRITUAL PATHS

There were two sides—the physical and the spiritual—of the LSD trip and what happened in the Haight: The media got a hold of the sex side and ignored the spiritual aspect of the acid trip.

—*Jay Thelin*

Our terminology was always getting high, expanding consciousness, always kind of a spiritual search . . . to embrace a higher consciousness. Then (after the media coverage and arrival of outsiders) the terminology became getting f upped, getting wasted. That wasn't what my core group of people wanted to do . . . so when that happened and the drugs got harder, the creative energy left and many of us left Haight-Ashbury.

—*Eric Christensen*

My first experience with spirituality was with LSD when I was 17.

—*Deepak Chopra*

Two Harvard professors, Timothy Leary and Richard Alpert originally experimented with LSD for scientific research on affecting behavior in beneficial ways, thinking they could help alcoholics and criminals. Many of the

participants who took LSD spoke of mystical and spiritual experiences, and in 1966 Leary founded the League of Spiritual Discovery, a religion with LSD as its holy sacrament. While touring college campuses he encouraged others to form their own psychedelic religions.

The spiritual experience of taking LSD prompted many hippies to look deeper for life's meaning and this led some to study spiritual writings—both old and new. Five books on spirituality, in particular, were favored by the hippies: *The Fellowship of the Ring* (Tolkien), *I Ching*, *The Tibetan Book of the Dead*, *Siddhartha* and *I and Thou*.

Of all the authors the hippies read, none was more beloved than Englishman J.R.R. Tolkien. Tolkien was a devout Roman Catholic who wrote most of his work between 1935 and 1966 (the year he helped translate the *Jerusalem Bible*). By May 1965, six months before the hippie movement began, approximately 214,000 copies of his novels had been sold worldwide. The hippies drew attention to Tolkien, and during and after the hippie movement,

sales of Tolkien's books took off. By 2010, approximately 90 million copies had been sold, 11 million in the U.S. alone. The *Lord of the Rings* trilogy, published in 1954 and 1955, has been a favorite among evangelical Christians for the last three decades, and is often referred to as a Christian novel. The three blockbuster movies made from the trilogy in 2001-2003 together grossed more than two billion dollars.

The hippies freely embraced teachings from any religion that made sense to them, and their admiration extended beyond Christian writers. The *Tibetan Book of the Dead*, an eighth-century Tibetan Buddhist text, first appeared in English translation in the 1920s, and the hippies became avid readers of it. They also loved the insights and oracular nature of the *I Ching*, or *Book of Changes*, an ancient Chinese divination system and text in the Confucius and Taoist traditions. Sales of the *Tibetan Book of the Dead* and the *I Ching* exploded after their reading became a "prerequisite" for passing Ken Kesey's Acid Tests between 1965 and 1967. Hippies read and memorized parts of both books, and held public readings to promulgate their ideas. Nearly one million copies of the *I Ching* have been sold since the mid-1960s. The *Tibetan Book of the Dead* has inspired numerous authors, including the hippie patriarchs, Timothy Leary and Richard Alpert/Ram Das, who used it as the basis for their book, *The Psychedelic Experience*. Leary's and Alpert's book itself has sold over a million copies and is in its thirty-seventh printing. Sogyal Rinpoche's *Tibetan Book of Living and Dying*, a reinterpretation of the classic Tibetan text published in 1994, has sold more than 2 million copies and has been published in thirty languages and fifty-nine countries.

The German-Swiss novelist Hermann Hesse's *Siddhartha*, a spiritual novel about Indian Buddhism, sold just four hundred copies in its first year of publication in English (1952), doubling to eight hundred the next year. When influential hippie leaders began quoting passages from it in the mid-1960s, sales of *Siddhartha* rocketed, and, it started selling a quarter of a million copies a year. By the early 1970s, 15 million copies of the book had been sold.

Jewish theologian Martin Buber's book, *I and Thou*, written in 1923, also became very popular among the hippies. When Dave Rothkop, a philosophy professor and hippie business owner, opened his coffee shop in 1966 at 1736 Haight Street, he called it the I and Thou Coffee Shop. Today, Buber's book

I and Thou coffee shop

is considered a classic text in Jewish spirituality, standard reading for seminarians and other students of philosophy and religion. Prior to the hippies, *I and Thou* had a tiny readership. Since the mid-1960s, *I and Thou* has steadily sold approximately 120,000 copies annually.

In summary, sales of the *I Ching, The Tibetan Book of the Dead, Siddhartha, I and Thou*, and the works of Tolkien have totaled over $300 million since the mid-1960s, when the hippie movement began. The proselytizing Haight-Ashbury hippies not only incorporated the principles of these works into their personal philosophies, but unashamedly encouraged others to do the same.

The hippies did the same with yoga and meditation, two spiritual practices that had been around for thousands of years. As early as 1893, Swami Vivekananda was promoting the benefits of yoga at the World's Fair in Chicago. "In America is the place, the people, the opportunity for everything new," he wrote before embarking on his journey from India to the United States. By 1961 there was already a television series, "Yoga and Health," but it took the hippies—who fully embraced the spiritual aspects of yoga and meditation, who were searching for higher consciousness—to integrate these practices into their lifestyle and spread the word. The hippies attraction to yoga and meditation were influenced by many spiritual leaders including Swami Satchidananda, who founded the Integral Yoga Institute, Suzuki Roshi, who founded the San Francisco Zen Center, Swami Kriyananda, and Dr. Haridas Chaudhri. With missionary furor, the hippies' religious and spiritual enthusiasms would ultimately infiltrate the mainstream and influence not only how millions of non-hippies exercised and relaxed but how they perceived organized religion, including the country's most prominent one: Christianity.

THE HIPPIES AND JESUS

One wall (in the hippie pad) was covered with pictures of Buddha, Christ, Saint Francis, a Red Indian Chief, some Hindu swami, Allen Ginsberg, the Grateful Dead, Bob Dylan, and some others . . .

—*Toni Del Renzio,* **The Flower Children**

The "Shroud of Turin" had a very big impact on the hippies in the Haight. That's because it showed Christ not as some beautiful person, but as he really once was. We were fascinated with that shroud. It had an element of reality to it. It wasn't a plastic rendering, some American artist's rendition of Jesus, but the real man.

—*Jay Thelin*

Many of the hippies were deeply spiritual, and an important star of their spiritual universe was Jesus Christ. They believed his teachings should be literally applied to their lives. The hippies were in love with Jesus, not the Christian religion or the Christian Church. Their rejection of institutional-ized Christianity clearly fell in line with the iconoclastic nature of the move-ment, but it wasn't rebellion for its own sake. By the mid-sixties, many religious institutions had either lost sight of their original missions or had embraced causes that did not resonate with the average believer. For exam-ple, by 1965, many mainline Protestant churches had all but lost the notion of personal spirituality, having turned their attention to social justice issues of the day.

While admirable, church ministries that were heavily focused on Martin Luther King's fight against racism, John Kennedy's "ask not" voluntarism, and Lyndon Johnson's war on poverty often fell short of meeting parishioners' need for a gospel that spoke to their personal hungers and particular situa-tions. In contrast, personal religion was a hallmark of hippie spirituality, and it enjoyed a warm reception, not just from Protestants, but Catholics, too.

American Evangelicalism and the Charismatic Movement made strong in-roads into both Protestant and Catholic faith communities, thanks to re-ligious firebrands like Billy Graham and Oral Roberts, who preached a highly personal and private gospel that centered on the individual's soul. Sixties' evangelicals and charismatic Christian leaders preached an individualistic and close reading of the gospel which rang true with many hippies, who took Jesus' teachings—such as "love your enemy" and "do good to those who would harm you"—not only seriously, but literally. The hippies' smorgasbord approach to Christianity ran the gamut from the ironically goofy (an early hippie button said "Jesus is God's Atom Bomb") to the overblown (in a July

1967 *Time Magazine* article, Bishop James Pike compared the hippies to the early Christians) to the shallow (Burton Wolfe writes that Chet Helms, "like so many hippie men, was obsessed with a Jesus self-image"). More than a few hippie males sported long hair, beards, flowing white robes and hippie sandals commonly referred to as "Jesus boots."

The hippies' infatuation with Jesus Christ was not frivolous, and many hippies were changed for good once they had been "born-again." These new Christian hippies led changed lives while still embracing many hippie values, which ultimately affected not only how they practiced their new-found faith but also how they worshipped. Unconventional at the time, Christian hippies introduced new worship forms that today, ironically enough, are adopted by thousands of the country's most conservative Christian congregations.

WORSHIPTAINMENT

Electric music is very important to the younger generation. It would do some of these old people good too.

—*Pastor Cecil Williams*

The collapse of Haight-Ashbury did not bring a collapse of the youth movement. Some youth went into rural communes. Others adopted new religions . . . of a Christian fundamentalist variety . . .

—*John Howard,* **The Cutting Edge**, *1974*

Folk/rock music and the hang-loose style that have become the preferred mode of church worship in many American churches today can be traced to a specific time and place: a San Francisco church, still located at 330 Ellis Street, where on a Sunday morning in March 1967, a bunch of hippies and a Christian pastor willing to take a huge risk, sponsored the first hippie worship service, giving birth to a billion-dollar industry we know today as contemporary Christian music and worship.

In 1963, twenty-three-year-old Cecil Williams accepted his first pastoral position at Glide Memorial United Methodist Church located in San Francisco's poorest neighborhood, the Tenderloin District, not far from Haight-Ashbury. His mission was not just to hippies, but to all, particularly social outcasts. He preached acceptance at all levels: hippie and non-hippie, gay and straight, black and white, alcoholics, addicts, and others left out of the American mainstream. According to Jay Thelin, "Cecil Williams was remarkable. He brought Christian truth and ideals to San Francisco. He was greatly affected by the Diggers and began to create social programs of ministry in the Tenderloin. I believe the Haight-Ashbury had a profound effect on his ministry."

Back in 1966 Reverend Williams was struggling. Just three years into his ministry, a substantial number of his congregation had left, turned off by his willingness to accept any and all to worship. All through the spring and summer of 1966, Williams took to the streets to actively minister to Haight-Ashbury hippies. Initial attempts at bringing them into the church failed, because they were reluctant to attend a Sunday morning service. So Williams invited them to a weekend event, essentially turning over the church facilities to them. Attendees quickly got high, shed their clothes, and danced. After twelve hours, the event was shut down. A less courageous pastor might have called it quits at that point, but Williams persisted.

The first "contemporary Christian worship service," took place when he invited hippies to come as they were and join the Sunday morning worship, which he called "A Welcome to the Pilgrims—A Celebration of Being Born Free." To make his guests feel welcome, Pastor Williams acquired electric guitars and amplifiers, greeting hippie worshipers not with centuries-old German and British hymns, but with the sounds of their own folk-rock music, some laced with Christianized lyrics. Formality was out. Worshipers were encouraged to sing, dance, and share—shirts and shoes optional. The Church was packed and the hippies danced, fully clothed this time with lyrics strong on love—the love of Jesus. This was the first time anyone had conducted such a Christian worship service.

Many worship formats and music styles have come and gone in the years since. What gave this particular style of Christian music and worship the legs to stand the test of time? This much we know: had it been left only to Pastor Williams and the Glide congregation, contemporary Christian worship/music would probably have never left the Bay Area, much less become the national sensation that it is today. But it did—hippie folk-rock music and worship services moved quickly from northern to southern California—a move that may be attributed to a group of hippie wannabes who arrived during and immediately after the original Haight-Ashbury hippies and referred to themselves as "Jesus freaks."

JESUS FREAKS

Jesus freaks had the same outer appearance of most hippies, but inside, something had changed. They had experienced a metamorphosis that the great psychologist William James wrote about some eighty years earlier, an experience as old as humankind itself: spiritual conversion. The Jesus freaks took the infatuation that some of the original hippies had with Jesus's appearance and teachings to a whole new level: they made a personal commitment to Jesus and became born-again. To express their new-found faith, they used the worship style originated by Williams and a small Haight-Ashbury storefront —The Living Room—founded by Ted and Liz Wise.

The Living Room was to the Jesus Movement what Glide Memorial Methodist Church was to contemporary Christian music and worship—its point of origin. Ted and Liz Wise, like Cecil Williams, were born-again Christians before they arrived in the Haight, but unlike Williams, their focus was consistently on strong evangelical objectives. William's role was to save, too—not just lost souls, but the socially lost—from the mean streets, drug addiction, and ostracism. Yet Williams and the Wises shared Christian values, a personal belief in Jesus, and principles that endorsed alternative styles of Christian worship and music. Their combined efforts were soon felt throughout the country.

After the Haight-Ashbury hippies got a hold of it, contemporary Christian worship focused on God, the music and the experience. Today, the worship is enhanced by electric music, amplifiers, and multi-media light shows in some of the country's best-attended entertainment venues: mega-churches. A new worship format that places music front and center, the contemporary Christian service has become either the Sunday morning main event or an alternative worship choice for thousands of American churches and millions of American worshipers. The commercial outcome of this blend of hippie and Christian spirituality is another billion dollar industry.

SUMMARY

Many counterculture groups embrace spiritual beliefs, but most do not spur strong and widespread consumer demand for their holy writs, spiritual novels, and music. Indeed, they are often mocked or even condemned by the mainstream. The hippies have been mocked and condemned for their drugs, long hair and slovenly look, however their spiritual products and endorsements have proven viral power. Yoga and meditation are now part of everyday life for millions of Americans. The spiritual writings, songs, books, and symbols adopted or created by hippies and the Jesus freaks filled a longing to feed the soul and to get closer to God. Americans, it seems, were ready for religious change, and the hippies were catalysts, formulating an amalgam of two-thousand-year-old teachings by Jesus Christ and hippie ideals preached by "freaks" on the streets of Haight-Ashbury in the mid-1960s.

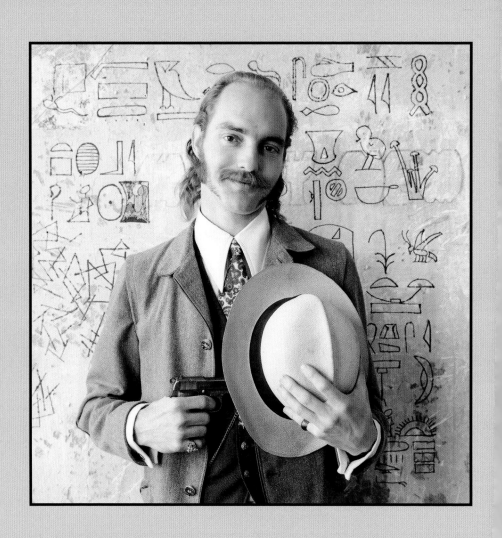

PART V

*

ORIGINALS

Frid 67

TICKET OUTLETS: DENVER: BRILLIG WORKS (2431 S. UNIVERSITY), POSTERS & THINGS (1215-15th, LARIMER SQUARE), HOBBIT BOOKSHOP LTD. (309 COLUM-
BINE, CHERRY CREEK), DENVER FOLKLORE CENTER (608 E. 17th), BOB OWENS KUSTOM MUSIC CO. (6403 E. COLFAX), JERRY'S NEWS (COLFAX
& BROADWAY), ARVADA PLAZA MUSIC (9518 W. 58th AVE, ARVADA, 2ND FLOOR ZOO (2510 W. MAIN, LITTLETON). BOULDER: CLANCY'S BOOKSHOP
(1322 COLLEGE), PHANTASMOGORIA (1310 COLLEGE). COLORADO SPRINGS: CEREBRAL CIRCUS (113 E.COSTILLA). FT. COLLINS: THE ESTAB-
LISHMENT (326-4 WALNUT).

No. D14.1   1967 © FAMILY DOG PRODUCTIONS, 639 GOUGH ST., San Francisco, Calif 94102

10

JOURNEY'S END

THE EARLY HAIGHT-ASHBURY hippies were originals. They were nonconformists, free thinkers, and in a community of about 800 people there was an abundance of talent and creativity. Selecting which hippies to profile in this book was subjective and difficult because so many of them have made an impact on our culture. The people highlighted in this chapter contributed greatly to Hippie, inc.

ROBERT DENNIS CRUMB

A descendant of President Andrew Jackson, Robert Dennis Crumb (a.k.a. R. Crumb) began drawing comics and selling them door to door as a child. He got his first job in 1962 at the age of nineteen, working as a greeting card artist with American Cards. Off-hours he socialized with a group of young bohemians and composed one of the earliest books of the graphic novel genre, which tells a narrative in comic book form. *Big Yum Yum Book* (1963) introduced one of his most beloved characters, Fritz the Cat, and offered his trademark biting social commentary.

After dropping acid in 1966 Crumb found his greeting card job unendurable and, at the urging of his wife, they moved to San Francisco. There he used the proceeds of his early successes to found Zap Comix in 1967 on Haight Street.

Robert was an incredible illustrator. He had two brothers who drew comics. The late Charles Crumb was the best of the brothers. Max was brilliant too. Somehow these brothers had the comic gene. Even as kids, they were drawing. Crumb had this incredible eye-hand coordination. I never saw anything like it. He would walk around with a sketch pad and draw from whatever angle he happened to be . . . He has the extraordinary skill to replicate what he sees and give it back to you unfettered.

—*Ron Turner*

In 1993 Crumb moved with his family to southern France, where he still lives. Aside from making a fortune for himself, Crumb succeeded in kick-starting the now-thriving graphic narrative genre that had combined sales in Canada and the U.S. worth $395 million in 2011. Today, Crumb is best known for his "Keep on truckin'" series as well as his cover design for Janis Joplin's "Cheap Trick" album. One of his most significant contributions to American commerce is having created some of the first adult cartoons in the U.S.A. (adult cartoons had already been in Europe for decades).

DEL CLOSE

Del Close, a Merry Prankster, was the stage manager for the San Francisco improvisational company, The Committee.

Del Close is my biggest influence in comedy.

—*John Belushi*

Building on the early work of Viola Spolin and her Los Angeles-based Young Actors Company, he laid down the foundations of modern-day improvisational comedy or "improv," becoming the director of Chicago's Second City, and joining *Saturday Night Live* in the eighties. He developed a seminal long-form type of improv, which he named the "Harold" and went on to mentor many of the best-known modern comedians including John Belushi, Chris Farley, Gilda Radner, Bill Murray, Amy Poehler, and Tina Fey. He also acted in the movies "Ferris Bueller's Day Off" and "The Untouchables."

LAUREL BURCH

Laurel Burch was an artist and designer of distinctive, colorful jewelry. Her story is a rags-to-riches drama with a hippie twist. She ran away from an unhappy home at fourteen; by twenty she was a single mother of two, trying to stretch her welfare check by fashioning jewelry out of found objects, in the kitchen of her Haight-Ashbury apartment. She began selling the creations on the street from a fishing tackle box. Without any formal education, she also taught herself to paint—fantastic, multicolored creatures, moons, and especially cats. She went on to found three multi-million dollar companies: Laurel Burch Designs, Laurel, Inc., Laurel Burch.

Tsvi Strauch and his wife Hyla were the first retailers to pick up on Burch's talent and began to stock her jewelry. A few more shops in the Haight began to offer her jewelry. One day it caught the eye of an Indian businessman passing through. Eventually, after she traveled to China to learn the art of cloisonné, that businessman gave Burch the financial backing to start manufacturing her designs. Eventually, Laurel Burch designs were sold in thousands of stores around the world on everything from tote bags to jewelry to mugs. *Forbes* magazine in 1985 said she "had created a niche between high-volume, low-price costume jewelry and high-priced designer lines like Paloma Picasso's."

TOM DONAHUE

Tom "Big Daddy" Donahue was a disc jockey and rock and roll entrepreneur. He was a founder and partner in Autumn Records, a manger of several rock groups, and the owner of the San Francisco psychedelic nightclub Mothers. He also was a producer of the last public appearance of the Beatles, which took place at Candlestick Park in 1966. However, his most striking accomplishment was his transformation of how music was played on radio. After writing an article in *Rolling Stone* magazine—"AM Radio is dead and its Rotting Corpse is Stinking up the Airways"—he took over programming at KMPX, introduced "Freeform" radio where DJs selected tracks from albums and he put FM radio on the map. FM at the time was on a significantly lower rung than AM. But with better high fidelity and Donahue's liberated format, FM took off, eventually surpassing AM.

Whether it be radio or comedy or adult comics or food or fashion or spirituality or sustainability or music or mind expansion or yoga or meditation or online networks or acceptance of others, the original hippies had a broad and profound effect on the culture. Their ideas, products and preferences are now rooted in our everyday lives.

DISCIPLES

The original hippies influenced thousands of other talented people who became hippie disciples. These disciples incorporated many of the ideas and values of the counter-culture and went on to achieve astounding success in business, transforming old industries and creating new ones. The hippie disciples migrated to a variety of enterprises, from television to real estate to media to wind farms to technology and almost everything in-between. **Ben Cohen** and **Jerry Greenfield (Ben & Jerry)** took their counter-culture values and helped re-create the ice cream business. Haight-Ashbury resident **Charles Hall**, a graduate student at San Francisco State, invented the waterbed. Kinkos print shops was founded by **Paul Orfalea**, a Santa Barbara hippie who eventually sold the franchises to Fed Ex in 2004 for $2.4 billion. Seattle hippies **Murray Pletz, Skip Yowell, and Jan Lewis** founded Jansport in 1967 and it is now the world's largest backpack company. Skip Yowell, years later, wrote the book *The Hippie Guide to Climbing the Corporate Ladder and other Mountains.* The hippie disciple who more than any other climbed the corporate ladder was **Steve Jobs.** He was too young to be an original hippie but he grew up in

Mountain View, in the heart of Silicon Valley, and a midway point between Haight-Ashbury and Santa Cruz. He was heavily influenced by both the technology and hippie cultures. The distance from Mountain View to Menlo Park (where Ken Kesey was experimenting with LSD when Jobs was a child) is an eight mile almost straight line along El Camino Real. The distance from Hippie, inc. to Jobs is also an almost straight line. Jobs grew his hair long, embraced the counter culture, took LSD, changed his diet to hippie foods, dropped out of college, ran an apple orchard at a commune, read *Be Here Now* by Ram Das and made a spiritual quest to India—a hippie path to enlightenment. While in India he met Larry Brilliant (who would become Stewart Brand's partner in The WELL). In Walter Isaacson's great biography of the founder and leader of Apple, *Steve Jobs,* he quotes Jobs as saying, "I came of age at a magical time . . . Our consciousness was raised by Zen and also by LSD . . . Taking LSD was a profound experience, one of the most important things in my life. LSD shows you that there's another side of the coin . . . It reinforced my sense of what was important—creating great things instead of making money, putting things back into the stream of history and of human consciousness as much as I could." In 2011 the BBC made a documentary about Jobs which they aptly titled *Steve Jobs: Billion Dollar Hippy.*

11

HOW DID THEY DO IT?

I am amazed at how much of the stuff I experienced back then is still with me 50 years later. Like competition . . . in my business today, I would rather collaborate than compete—I don't see any reason for a businessperson like me to try to destroy my competition. Another thing, acceptance . . . I am surprised that so few people have yet to learn to give the other person the benefit of the doubt. That was what we believed—you are different from me but you are just as valid as me. The collegiality that we tried to engender . . . the willingness to let people do their own thing without judgment—it just makes sense, it makes good business sense.

—Mark Braunstein

DIVERSE IN THEIR membership, hippie leaders held several characteristics in common that led to the remarkable success of the products they endorsed and their innovations.

1. **Proactivity:** Before the word became popular with business management experts, the hippies were taking the initiative and "getting the jump." The desire to seize the day coupled with a passion to do the *right* thing extended to their choice of livelihoods as they spurned traditional career paths with guaranteed financial benefits and opted instead to open their own shops, and experiment with

product alterations. They became the "first movers," to offer, for example, psychedelic rock posters and cutting-edge fashions. Jumping ahead of the pack is a highly prized business position. By the time most of the country's business leaders first heard about yogurt, camouflage clothing, and love beads, the commercial beachhead was squarely in place. Similar to Silicon Valley and the hi-tech industry, Haight-Ashbury became the geographical locus of the country's next fashion, food, and health trends, as long-haired young Americans took over the control seat, commanding the design, sales, and distribution of their products.

2. **Preparation**: Hippie Fred Rohe worked as a stacker at a health food store in the city, before creating the prototype of the modern-day organic/natural grocery store modeled by Trader Joe's and Whole Foods. Art student, Wes Wilson, spent hours in libraries and galleries drawing inspiration from the techniques of early-20th and late-19th century German and Austrian painters before inventing the psychedelic motif. Light show originator Bill Ham said he spent almost no time in Haight-Ashbury: "I arrived at the theater early in the morning and went home well after midnight." Laughing, he added: "There was little time for me to be a hippie, for me, being an artist was a full-time endeavor." Even questionable commercial activity was preceded by thought and method: chemist Augustus Owsley discovered his LSD recipes in the UC-Berkeley Science Library and ended up selling approximately 1.25 million doses of the highest-grade acid ever cooked. And if there was ever a hippie with a studied approach, it was Stewart Brand, an inventor and founder of the first online interactive community.

3. **Capital**: Even the best ideas are unlikely to succeed if not backed with sufficient capital investment. The hippies drew from four primary sources: drug profits, state and federal subsidies (i.e., unemployment and welfare checks), personal fortunes, and family assistance. During the mid-to late sixties, welfare checks could be as much as $400 per month, which was plenty of money for a per-

son to get by on in those pre-inflationary days. Not all hippies, despite espousing libertarian ideals, resisted the largesse of the Great Society. Nor did many of these people consider selling drugs to be ethically wrong. Those with access to capital were able to provide start-up money and cash-flow for ongoing business operation expenses, and invested in new enterprises, including several small hippie-owned businesses, a few of which eventually made millions and employed hundreds of people.

4. **Reinvention**: Almost everything the hippies introduced was either a renewed appreciation for existing but forgotten products, such as whole-grain bread or yogurt, a revision of established traditions, such as Christian music and worship, or the creative use of emerging technology that enhanced an existing industry, such as using the newest printing processes (developed during the 1960s) to mass produce and distribute posters and t-shirts. Working with what was already available afforded an opportunity to turn new ideas into reality quickly and with minimal starting costs.

5. **Pragmatism**: Hippie leaders were *economic and political pragmatists.* The fact that most hippies are today identified with the far-left wing of the Democratic Party is more likely a reflection of the later student radicals and their causes than the early Haight-Ashbury hippies and their interests. Many of the early hippie businesspeople were neither Democrat nor Republican, but libertarian. Some were anarchists and others were apolitical. They believed that Americans should be left to lead their lives and businesses as they pleased, with as little government intervention as possible. As for the production and sale of products—whether of candy bars or hallucinogenic drugs—hippies believed that consumers, not government officials, should have the right to decide what will and will not be for sale.

6. **Principles**: Many hippie entrepreneurs insisted on marketing their creations and conducting their ventures in *a principled manner.* In other words, they shared *a strong sense of personal and social*

responsibility, and urgency, for solving the social and economic problems of their local community. Judy Goldhaft and Jodi Robbin, for example, could have made millions when they adopted the ancient practice of Shibori and created the first tie-dye shirt. But that was never their goal. This story repeated itself many times in the space of those one hundred weeks: smart, often well-educated, creative people driven by a singular purpose to make the world a better place, with little or no thought to how they might personally benefit, came up with effective solutions that ultimately morphed into billion-dollar products and ideas. Often rejected, hippies refused to take their ball and go home. Instead they responded with quick and proactive intervention, turning failure into opportunity. Hippie business leaders and owners frequently spearheaded efforts to make the Haight community a better place to live—from organizing trash pickups of garbage that the city refused to collect, to creating business associations that welcomed businesspeople of color who had been rejected by other business associations in the city, to creating formal social and medical systems to deal with the problems of drug addiction and poverty that beset parts of their neighborhood, to forming councils in anticipation of the chaotic situations that usually accompanied mass gatherings in the neighborhood, such as "the summer of love." This can-do spirit and the refusal to sit back and wait for others encouraged more businesses to open, attracting a diversity of owners and customers. Research and common sense suggest that organizations and leaders who live and operate with conviction and an uncompromising set of principles tend to fare better than those who move from one thing to the next without a philosophical or moral compass. Sometimes the guiding philosophies of businesspeople are founded in religious belief and spirituality. Clear principles coupled with spiritual sensibility provided some Haight business leaders with a sense of "calling," a compulsion to evangelize and convince others, and a commitment to objectives that far surpassed the goal of simply making more and more money.

7. **Influence**: The original hippies were surprised by the response of American youth, or "the teeny-boppers," as Jay Thelin, referred to them in an interview. Already well into their twenties and beyond, most early hippie leaders were hoping to change their parents' minds, not the minds of their baby brothers and sisters. Nevertheless, they wasted no time in nurturing commercial relationships with younger buyers, introducing them not only to new products, but also new ideas—such as "Do your own thing"—that especially resonated with young people in the process of self-discovery. There was really no way that they could have known it, but the hippies were inadvertently rearing one of the most lucrative generations of the Great American Consumer. Huge in numbers, the boomers would change everything, and the hippies were in the enviable position of being their taste-makers, fashion editors, entertainment critics, and opinion leaders. In retrospect, it's clear that most Haight products would have never left the neighborhood, let alone entered into millions of American homes, had it not been for young boomers. The first generation of hippie wannabes (or "plastic hippies" as the early hippies called the imitators who followed them) were important influencers who shaped the consumer tastes and choices of future generations—what they would wear, eat, and listen to. The sheer size of this group insured that there would be a second, a third, and a fourth generation of counterculture consumers to follow. Baby boomers have helped cement the commercial legacy of the Haight-Ashbury hippies over the last five decades.

8. **Promotion**: Ford Motor understood early on that giving product away was a sound promotion strategy. During the national rollout of their Mustang in 1962, Ford gave away dozens of cars to people in positions of widespread influence: radio DJs, newspaper editors, and airline stewardesses who had daily contact with people nationwide. The method behind this madness reasoned that these influential people would tell others and the money lost initially would be more-than-made-up in later sales. From free concerts, to free universities, to free acid, the hippies handed out potentially

millions of dollars of products—and it paid off. The other "free" that really worked to the hippies benefit was all the free promotion that the media showered on them. As Burton Wolfe pointed out in *The Hippies,* "Shortly after the World's First Human Be-in was held in January of 1967, newspapers, magazines, and television stations from California to New York began zeroing in on the Haight-Ashbury. Never has there been such a publicized underground or subculture of any sort as the hippies. It was as though the entire communications media was mesmerized by this baffling revolution in life style. . . . It was the press that built the hippie movement into one of the major events of the twentieth century. . . . Without the free publicity agents, the hippies could not have made so great an impact. There might not even have been a term such as 'hippies.'" *Time, Life, Look,* and *The Atlantic* were just some of the major national magazines that did stories on them. FM Radio and national TV shows like the Smothers Brothers promoted hippie values and had high Nielsen ratings. The comedian George Carlin created the character of the Hippy Dippy Weatherman who was goofy, funny, and appealing.

9. **Teamwork**: Hippie ingenuity often sprang from the contributions of an eclectic, if not unorthodox, *team of talented people.* For example, psychedelic posters relied on the talents of graphic artists, musicians, promoters, and skilled printers, and light shows combined the visual artists with musicians and audience participants. The same is true today for innovative businesses. Bill Gates and Steve Jobs were brilliant individuals but the success of their companies relied on teams working cohesively and creatively together, and quite often, outside the box.

10. **Place**: Esteemed Professor, Richard Florida, argues in his best-selling book, *The Rise of the Creative Class,* that geographical location is an important factor in commercial success. His research suggests, creative people move to where other creative people live—and, creative companies follow suit. As Florida points out, since the

Greek Empire, creative people have tended to congregate in cities, like Athens, Rome, Paris, and New York. Haight-Ashbury was perfectly positioned between the location of two of the most influential youth movements in American history (North Beach beats and Berkeley campus radicals) and was in a location that enjoyed a 12-month growing season, permitting year-long access to the fresh fruits and vegetables that were hippie staples and main ingredients in their billion-dollar food innovations. The Haight was also surrounded by universities and colleges, some like Stanford and Berkeley being internationally acclaimed institutions. The neighborhood existed a stone's throw from one of the most desirable harbors in the world that had played host to commercial vessels for decades and become the center of U.S. export and import activities. Professor Florida has crowned San Francisco as the most creative city in the U.S.

AUTHOR'S PERSONAL REFLECTION
—FIFTY YEARS LATER

You see, my life and all my businesses are all the outcome of the hippie philosophy. These businesses and my lifestyle, my spirituality—all these are the fruit of those days in the Haight.

—*Jay Thelin*

When my wife and I set out on what was to become a 8-year journey, we had no idea that we would become connected to so many interesting and intriguing people. Born in 1953 and 1954, Emily and I were both influenced by the ideas and ideals of the hippie movement starting shortly after we left home for college in 1972. (I actually visited Haight-Ashbury in the summer of 1968, pathetically enough, as a tourist with my parents.) Having been issued my draft number, I joined with my fellow college students to learn more about the Vietnam War, and what I learned made me conclude that—despite a proud family history of military service—I could not conscientiously support the war, let alone participate in it. Fortunately, the war was brought to a close shortly after I entered college, but the ideas I adopted from my fellow students and members of the campus Peace Club, to which I belonged, have stuck with me to this day.

Once we finished college, Emily and I moved to California where we sought to live as simply and non-materialistically as possible. We became vegetarians and participated in the few campus protests that were still taking place in the late-1970s. When we moved into our first professional positions, we continued to share living quarters and possessions with others, even though it was not financially necessary to do so. The birth of our three children and the demands of two careers made it more difficult to live simply, but we never forgot what we had learned. Buying locally, thinking globally, and supporting projects of peace and justice, we did our best to convey the values we had adopted in young adulthood to our kids.

In my personal memory, real hippies were people to be looked up to. When I thought about them I was not prone to conjure up images of drugged-out slackers but sober and seriously smart people. My mind turned to people like David, who turned down the opportunity to attend Harvard to work in the inner city, and Bill, who, instead of copping a plea, elected to spend two years in jail for refusing to be drafted into the army. How did we end up forgetting the quiet, sincere believers and focusing all our attention instead on the stoners, the media hounds, and the wannabees? Today, old memories from high school and college have been supplemented with new memories of *authentic* Haight-Ashbury hippies, most now in their seventies. Today, when I think about the original hippies I'm awed by how much they accomplished, that one neighborhood, one subculture of 800 people, could be home to so many talented individuals.

Working in higher education for the last thirty-five years, I have come to believe that each generation of Americans offers us their own version of hippies. (These bright, young people may just as likely be wearing a suit and tie as a tie-dye shirt and sandals.) And while it is okay—and sometimes the best thing to do—to reject the ideas and ideals of American's latest crop of hippies, it is rarely a good idea to reject those ideas and their originators, outright. As we can see from the original hippies, though there were plenty of destructive elements within the hippie experience, there were also many fruitful ideas and products. This book's focus is on the commercial aspects of the hippie legacy and it is clear to me that a good business idea and a sure-fire product—backed up with some of the characteristics that helped the hippies achieve their success—will make tons of money for many people, no matter how long the inventor's hair is or how often he bathes, or how oddly she dresses or what blazing disc he wears on his forehead. It has taken decades to comprehend the scope of the contributions made to the country's economy and its workers by Hippie, inc., but the time has come to acknowledge the impressive legacy to our culture and our economy that the original hippies created.

APPENDICES

✳

Michael Klassen and Tsvi Strauch

APPRECIATION

I express appreciation to the University of Northern Iowa for reliable and generous support of this book. In particular, I am grateful to Gloria Gibson (former University of Northern Iowa Executive Vice President and Provost); Farzad Moussavi (Dean of the College of Business Administration); Christine Twait (Assistant Provost for Sponsored Programs); Randy Pilkington (Executive Director of Business and Community Services); Maureen Collins-Williams (former Director of Business and Community Services); Steven Corbin (former Marketing Department Head); and Matthew Bunker (Marketing Department Head).

I also express my thanks to those women and men who spent time with me, helping me get the facts right, including:

Bill Ham: Principle pioneer of music light shows

Bonnie MacLean: Psychedelic poster artist and former wife of Bill Graham

Burton Wolfe: Author of an early first-hand account of the hippies (*The Hippies*, 1968)

David Simpson: Digger hippie and actor

Eric Christiansen: Worked with Tom "Big Daddy" Donahue at KMPX, film documentaries-maker, and former ABC producer

Ernest Becker: Early Santa Cruz hippie

Fred Rohe: Organic and natural food retail pioneer (supermarkets, cafes, trade unions, and wholesale distribution)

George Hunter: Leader of the first hippie band, responsible for the Victorian/Cowboy look of the early hippies

Harvey Kornspan: Digger hippie, manager of The Steve Miller Band, and former CBS executive

Herb Greene: Important photographer of the San Francisco Music Scene

Jane Lapiner: Digger hippie responsible for making and distribution of whole-grain, artisan breads

Jay Thelin: Co-founder (with brother, Ron) of The Psychedelic Shop, which was the first hippie shop on Haight Street

Jeanne Rose: Master designer for the Jefferson Airplane among other well-known American rock groups; "godmother" of essential oils, herbalism, and aromatherapy industries; and author of 25 books on these topics

John Helms: Assistant to and brother of legendary promoter, the late Chet Helms

Judy Goldhaft: Originator, with Jodi Palladini, of tie-dye apparel

Julius Karpen: Business manager of Big Brother and the Holding Company (with Janis Joplin)

Lou Honary: Industrial inventor

Marilyn Strayer: Early Santa Cruz hippie

Mark Braunstein: Roadie for Big Brother and the Holding Company (with Janis Joplin), and the Kozmic Blues Band (with Joplin)

Mark McCloud: LSD historian

Merimee Moffatt: Early hippie and partner of Steve Mork (leader of ph factor jug band)

Nancy Van Brasch Kamren: Co-founder, Nancy's Yogurt

Penelope DeVries: Early hippie and, later, business owner

Robert Limon: Street kid during the Haight-Ashbury hippie movement

Ron Turner: Important publisher of underground "comix", including the work of R. Crumb

Sheryl Kesey Thompson: Niece of Ken Kesey and a manager of the Kesey Springfield Farm, producer of Nancy's Yogurt

Signe Anderson: Original female vocalist with Jefferson Airplane

Skip Yowel: Co-founder of Jansport, Inc.

Travis Rivers: Early hippie who worked closely with the Oracle newspaper

William Bisbee: Early hippie

I express special appreciation to Tsvi Strauch who generously shared his wealth of knowledge and contacts, and I pay tribute to his late wife, Hyla Deer Strauch. Both were an entrepreneurial team of the highest caliber who pioneered Uni-Sex attire and men's nontraditional jewelry and accessories before and during the hippie movement.

I thank my cameraman, Robb Klassen, his assistant, Kellie Kreiss, and my film producer, David O'Shields, and his assistant, Jacob Meade, for their valuable input with my videotaped interviews and forthcoming film. I express appreciation to my Web and Social Media directors, Weston Lohry and Darren Westervelt.

I express gratitude to my freelance editor, Nancy Doherty, who offered encouragement and helpful insights in the initial phase of this book. I also express thanks to my editors and publishers Andrew Goldstein and Michelle Toth. Andrew went well above the call of duty and I am grateful to have met him and have him as my publisher. I am thankful for Herbie Greene's involvement and his generosity in allowing me to use his wonderful photographs.

I am grateful to my wife, Emily Klassen, my traveling companion for the last 40 years who, thanks to her outgoing and charming manner, helped put me be in touch with folks that I would have otherwise missed. I am also thankful for the loving support of my children, Scott Klassen, Robb Klassen, and Jeni Klassen who have always helped give my life meaning and a sense of purpose.

(*Publisher's appreciation:* Mike Klassen has been a joy to work with, Chiquita Babb has been a great partner designing the interior of this book, Max Goldstein created the cover we were looking for, Lucy Goldstein added illustrations for the spine, Serena Howlett was a conscientious copyeditor, Stuart Horwitz from Book Architecture was as usual very insightful, Jeff Thomas from the San Francisco Public Library Historical Photographs Department was absolutely fabulous, Tsvi Strauch, as Mike has already acknowledged, contributed greatly to this book, and several people generously let us use their images free of charge, including the estate of Allen Cohen and Mark Weiman of Regent Press—publisher of the *San Francisco Oracle Facsimile Edition*—and the photographers James Mason and Dennis Maness.)

CREDITS

(photos, posters, images)

Bob Seidemann

Bob Seidemann

Page: 57

Chuck Gould

Chuck Gould Photography

Page: 115

Corbis

Bob Campbell/San Francisco Chronicle/Corbis

Page: 65

Corbis Stewart

Bill Young/San Francisco Chronicle/Corbis

Page: 65

Dennis Maness

Dennis Maness photography

Pages: 16, 85, 106, 112 (*top*), 137, 138

Emily Klassen

Page: 168

Graphic posters

Artwork by Victor Moscoso. © 1967, 1984, 1995 Rhino Entertainment Company. Used with permission. All rights reserved.

Pages: x, 40, 156

Artwork by Bob Schnepf. © 1967, 1984, 1995 Rhino Entertainment Company. Used with permission. All rights reserved.

Page: 134, back cover

Artwork by Robert Fried. © 1967, 1984, 1995 Rhino Entertainment Company. Used with permission. All rights reserved.

Page: 150

Pages: 2, back cover (Wes Wilson), 26 (Lee Conklin), 80 (David Singer), 92, 124 (Bonnie MacLean), 104 (Peter Bailey)

Herb Greene

Herb Greene Photography

Pages: ii, xiii, xiv,xviii, xxii, xxiii, xxiv, 6, 9, 15, 19, 21, 24, 35, 37, 38, 42, 44, 46, 47, 50, 52, 54, 59, 66, 67, 68, 72, 83, 84, 90, 108, 111, 112 (*bottom*), 117, 118, 120 (*bottom*), 123, 127, 129, 130, 132, 143, 148, 166

James Mason

James Mason photography

Pages: 28, 31

John Gorham

Page: 109

ORACLE images

Images which originally appeared in *The San Francisco Oracle* provided courtesy of the estate of Allen Cohen and Regent Press, publishers of *The San Francisco Oracle Facsimile Edition Digital Version* available at www.regentpress.net

Pages: 18 (Azul—Bob Simmons), 147

Rob Klassen

Inside flap back cover photo

San Francisco Library

SAN FRANCISCO HISTORY CENTER, SAN FRANCISCO PUBLIC LIBRARY

Pages: 87, 120 (*top*), 140

San Francisco Library D.M.

SAN FRANCISCO HISTORY CENTER, SAN FRANCISCO PUBLIC LIBRARY. "SFP51 Dennis Maness Summer of Love Collection"

Pages: 16, 85, 106, 112 (*top*), 137, 138

Victor Moscoso

Neon Rose 1967, www.victormoscoso.com

Page: 62

HIPPIE, INC., LEADERS
AND INFLUENCES

Alan Watts
Author and spiritual leader

Dr. Albert Hoffman
Inventor of LSD

Alex Horn
Actor and cult leader-Gurdjieff

Ali Akbar Khan
Indian sarod player

Allah Rakah
Indian tabla player

Allen Cohen, Steve Levine, and Max Scherr
Founders of *The San Francisco Oracle* and the Berkeley Barb

Allen Ginsberg, Gary Snyder, George Tsongas, Kenneth Patchen, Kenneth Rexroth, Lawrence Ferlinghetti, Lenore Kandel, Mark Linethal, and Ruth Weiss
Beat poets

All Saints Episcopal Church—Father Leon Harris
Home of Diggers' free bakery and Council for the Summer of Love

Alton Kelley,* Bonnie MacLean,* Gilbert Shelton, Greg Irons, Gut, Jack Jackson, Jim Blashfield Joe Gomez, Mac McGrew, Mari Tepper, Phil Hammond, Rick Griffin,* Robert Fried, Stanley J. Miller, Jr.* ("Mouse"), Steve Resnick, Terré, Tom Weller, Victor Moscoso,* and Wes Wilson*
Poster artists

Anne Porteus, Baron Wolman, Bob Schnepf, Bruce Conner, Clayton Lewis, David Richards, Don Buchla, Edmund Shea, Gerd Stern, Greg Irons, Herb Greene, James Melchert, Jim Marshall, Judith Pearlman, Mark Rothko, Marvin Lipofsky, Michael Bowen, Michael Frimkiss, Patrick Gleeson, Peter Voulkos, Ron Boise, Ron Nagle, and Steven F. Arnold
Artists, designers, photographers

Ashoke Fakir
Indian hippie spiritual leader

Augustus Owsley Stanley, III*
Early investor in hippie products and maker and distributor of LSD

Avrum Rubenstein, Billy Batman, Bob Stubbs,* Bobby Bowles and partner, Carol Batman, Chloe Ferguson, "Big Daddy" Eric Nord,* Lawrence Ferlinghetti, Michael Ferguson, Peggy Caserta, and S. Paul Gee
Early counterculture retailers whose businesses spanned the Neo-Beat and hippie eras

Baba Ram Dass, Burton Wolfe, Charles Perry, Deborah Wolfe, Jack Kerouac, Ken Babbs, Ken Kesey, Lawrence Ferlinghetti, Leonard Wolfe, Philip Lamantia, Philip Whalen, Robert Scheer, and Tom Wolfe
Writers

Ben Van Meter, Dan Bruhns, David and Helena LeBrun, Elias Romero, George Holden, Gerd Stern, Glen McKay, Kenneth Anger, Luther Green, Ray Andersen, Roger Hillyard, "San Andreas Fault," and Tony Martin
Light show artists and filmmakers

Bill Ham*
Pioneer of the music light show

Bishop (James) Pike
Episcopal Bishop of California-Grace Cathedral

Bobby Hutcherson, Boz Scaggs, Carlos Santana, Christopher Tree, Dan Hicks, Dave Getz, David LaFlamme, Denny Zeitlin, Dewey Redman, Dino Valenti, Donald Rafael Garrett, Dottie Ivory, Elvin Bishop, Grace Slick, Graham Nash, Harvey Mandel, Jack Casady, Jim Morrison, John Dawson, John Handy, John Hendricks, Keith Jarrett, Linda LaFlamme, Malachi, Mark Naftalin, Mickey Hart, Mike Bloomfield, Nick Gravenites, Phil Lesh, Ron Stallings, Sandy Bull, Signe Anderson, Sonny Simmons, and Steve Miller
Jazz, blues, and rock musicians

Bruce Bratton, David Oliver, Fred McPherson, Jerry Kamstra, Leon Tabory, Mike Walker, Paul Lee, Peter Demma, Ralph Abraham, Rojulio, and Ron Bevirt
Santa Cruz hippie leaders

Bubba Free John
Self-invented spiritual leader

Bud Steinhoff (The Purple Onion), Harvey Kornspan (The Committee, The Steve Miller Band), Lawrence Ferlinghetti (City Lights Bookstore), Matthew Katz (Moby Grape, Jefferson Airplane), Moe Moskowitz (Moe's Books, The Print Mint), Ronnie G. Davis (The S. F. Mime Troupe), and Zack Stewart (with Stewart Brand, Trips Festival)
Business managers

Chabad Tefilin Mobile
Jewish ritual on wheels

Chester Anderson
Founder, The Communications Company

Council For the Summer of Love
Organization formed to better the Haight-Ashbury community and mitigate problems arising out of influx of people coming to the Haight. Founded by Stanley McDaniels and Tsvi Strauch

Dave Rothkop, Faith Petric, Jean Paul Pickens, Joan Baez, John Dawson (a.k.a. Marmaduke), John Fahey, Lou Gottleib, Mayne Smith, Mimi Farina, Rita Weill, and Robbie Basho
Folk and bluegrass musicians

Del Close*
Director of The Committee, mentor of many of America's greatest comedians in the late-20th century, and an important developer of long-form improvisational theater

Diane Varsi, Gary Goodrow, Hamilton Camp, Larry Hankin, and Peter Coyote
Actors

Diggers Free Frame of Reference
Stores where goods were given away for free

Don Buchia
Pioneer of music synthesizers

E. Buckminster Fuller
Architect, inventor

Ed Sanders
Poet, singer, co-founder of the Fugs

Emmett Grogan* and Peter Cohon (a.k.a. Peter Coyote)
Two of the founders of the Diggers

Esalen Institute, Big Sur
Retreat center offering humanistic alternative education

Father Chiranjiva
Spiritual leader (some say a fake)

Frank Werber,* Bill Graham,* and Chet Helms*
Leading promoters of rock-and-roll, folk, psychedelic, and hippie folk-rock music concerts and industry

Fred Rohe*
Principle pioneer of the modern natural and organic foods industry

George B. Leonard
Editor at *Look* magazine. Founded meditation center in Mill Valley

George Hunter,* Jerry Garcia,* Bob Dylan, The Byrds, and the Beatles
Musicians who were critical in helping bridge traditional American folk and hippie folk-rock music genres

Glide Memorial Methodist Church—Rev. Cecil Williams
Origin of contemporary worship services—("worshiptainment")

Haight-Ashbury Free Medical Clinic—Dr. David E. Smith
Free medical clinic

Haight-Ashbury Switchboard—Al Rinker
Referral source and runaway assistance

HALO (Haight-Ashbury Legal Organization)—Brian Rohan and Michael Stepanian
Lawyers helping hippies

Hamilton Methodist Church
Diggers gave away free food

Happening House—Deborah and Leonard Wolf
Offered cultural activities, education, and medical care

Herb Caen
San Francisco Chronicle journalist who coined the term "Hippie"

Hillel Foundation Outreach—Rabbi David
Offered services to people in need

HIP—Haight-Ashbury Independent Proprietors
Association of hippie merchants—Founded by Tsvi Strauch and Ron Thelin

HIP Job Co-op—Peter Mackaness
Source of job referrals

House of Love and Prayer—Rabbi Shlomo Carlebach
Alternative synagogue

J. Tony Serra
Defense attorney

Jacob Needleman
Professor of philosophy

James Melchert and Martin Lipofsky
Ceramic and glass artists

Jane Lapiner* and the Digger Women
Pioneered modern-day whole wheat and artisan breads industry

Janis Joplin
Lead singer, Big Brother and the Holding Company

Jeanne Rose*
Fashion designer and leading pioneer in aromatherapy, essential oils, and herbalism

Jerry Mander
Hippie bail bondsman

Jerry and Esther Sealund
Owners of Far Fetched Foods—an early natural/organic food store

Jodi Palladini* and Judith Goldhaft*
Originators of tie-dyed clothing and fabrics

John White
Owner of The Weed Patch shop

Judy Duggan, Jeanne Rose, Linda Gravenites, Nancy Gurley, Terré, and Virginia Wolf
Designers and hippie fashionistas

Julius Karpen
Business manager, Big Brother and the Holding Company

Ken Kesey,* Timothy Leary, Allen Ginsberg, Alan Watts and Peter Berg
Intellectual forces behind the three central tenets of Haight-Ashbury hippie ethos and culture: LSD (Ken Kesey and Tomothy Leary), Eastern mysticism (Allen Ginsberg and Alan Watts), and social and political activism (Peter Berg)

Ken Warren—aka Father Ken Warren
Minister at Grace Cathedral

Laurel Burch*
Jewelry and clothing designer who became president of Laurel Burch, Inc., a multi-million dollar company

LeMar—Lowell Eggemeier and James R. White III
Legalize marijuana

Lenore Kandel
Neo-Beat and hippie poet

Marty Balin
Founder, Jefferson Airplane

Merry Pranksters
Pre-hippie anti-establishment group centered around Ken Kesey and psychedelic drugs

Methodist Street Ministry
Run by Rev. Bill Bigelow who was ministering to hippies on the street

Michael McClure
Beat poet and playwright

Millbrook
Timothy Leary's, Richard Alpert's, and Ralph Metzner's base of operations in New York

Moe Moskowitz
Pricing innovator in used books and and pioneer in the national distribution of pop posters

Nancy Van Brasch Hamren*
Industry pioneer of yogurt and probiotic products in the U.S.

Peter Albin
Founder of Big Brother and the Holding Company

Psychedelic rangers—Allen Cohen, Gene Anthony, Martine Bowen, Michael Bowen, Ron Thelin, and Tsvi Strauch
Organizers of Human Be-in

R. Crumb,* Gary Edson Arlington, Gilbert Shelton, Ron Turner, and Spain Rodriguez
Comix artists, owner of first comic book store in U.S., and principal publisher (Last Gasp Publications) of the American underground "Comix" industry

Radha Krishna Temple—founder, Bhaktivedanta Swami Prabhupada
Home to Hare Krishna sect

Ralph Metzner
Psychotherapist who worked with Timothy Leary and became a professor at the California Institute for Integral Studies

Ravi Shankar
Indian sitar player

Richard Alpert—aka Babba Ram Das
Author, spiritual teacher

Richard Baker
Spiritual teacher—successor to Suzuki Roshi at Zen Center

Richard Brautigan
Neo-Beat and hippie author

Robert Scheer
Author and editor-in-chief of *Ramparts* magazine

Ron McKernan
Founding member of the Grateful Dead

Ron* and Jay Thelin*
Founders of the country's first "head shop"

Ronnie Davis
Founder, San Francisco Mime Troupe

Samuel L. Lewis
Dancer

San Francisco Art Institute

San Francisco Bay Guardian—Bruce B. Brugmann and Jean Dibble
Alternative newspaper

San Francisco Dancers Workshop—Anna Halprin
Performances and education

San Francisco Poetry Center—Mark Linenthal
Poetry

San Francisco Tape Music Center—Tony Martin, Morton Subotnick, and Ramon Sender
Concerts and education

San Francisco Zen Center—Founder, Suzuki Roshi
Zen study

Seymour Locks
Creator of liquid light shows

SFSU Free University
Free classes

Shlomo Carlebach
Rabbi, musician, and founder of The House of Love and Prayer

Stephen Gaskin
Spiritual leader and founder of "The Farm" commune

Steven Krolik, Ken Rand, Yvonne Rand, and Maharishi Mahesh Yogi
Pioneers in yoga, meditation, and Zen. Maharishi Mahesh Yogi was the founder of Transcendental Meditation (TM)

Steward Brand*
Creator of the *Whole Earth Catalogue* and one of the first virtual communities—The WELL

Swami Kriyananda
American spiritual teacher

Swami Satchidinanda
Indian spiritual teacher

Swami Sivinanda
Indian spiritual teacher

Terrance Hallinan
Civil rights activist and defense attorney

The Living Room—Ted and Liz Wise
Home of the Jesus Movement

The Realist—Paul Krassner
Alternative newspaper

Timothy Leary
Psychologist, writer, and advocate of psychedelic drugs

Tom "Big Daddy" Donahue*
Established FM Radio as a major advertising force and developed one of America's first alternative "free-form" radio stations (San Francisco KMPX)

Tony Martin
Owner of the San Francisco Tape Music Center

Trunga Ripoche
Teacher of Tibetan Buddhism

Tsvi (Harry) Strauch* and Hyla Davidovich Deer Strauch*
Premier retailers of non-traditional mens's jewelry and unisex accessories

Tuli Kupferberg
Poet and musician who was one of the founders of The Fugs

Walking Buddha
Took hippies on hikes as meditation

Wallace Bierman
L.A. Neo-Beat artist had strong influence on hippie artists

Warren Hinckle, Jr.
Journalist, executive editor at *Ramparts* magazine

Wavy Gravy
Entertainer

*profiled in *Hippie, Inc.*

REFERENCES

www.census.gov

www.EPA.gov

www.FDA.com

www.USDA.gov

www.google.com/ngrams

www.barna.org

www.diggers.org

www.organicconsumers.org

www.travel–goods.org

www.businessoffashion.com

www.teausa.com

http://home.packagedfacts.com

www.statisticbrain.com

www.comichron.com

www.faithcommunitiestoday.org

www.chickenonaunicycle.com

Aiden, E. and Michel, J. (2013). *Uncharted*, NY: Riverhead Books

Cook, Roberta (2008). "Trends in the marketing of fresh produce and fresh-cut products," University of California-Davis.

Goins, D. (1993). *The Free Speech Movement*, Berkeley, CA: Ten Speed Press

Grogan, Emmett. (1972). *Ringolevio: A Life Played for Keeps.* New York: New York Review Books.

Gruen, John. (1966). *The New Bohemia: The Combine Generation.* New York: Shorecrest, Inc.

History of the Erewhon—Natural Foods Pioneers in the United States 1966–2011, Soyinfo Center, 2011.

Howe, Irvin (Ed.). (1966). *The Radical Papers.* Garden City, NY: Anchor Books

Howe, Irving and Harrington, Michael. (1972). *The Seventies.* New York: Harper & Row.

Hopkins, Jerry (Ed.) (1968). *The Hippie Papers.* New York: Signet Books.

Howard, John R. (1974). *The Cutting Edge.* New York: J.B. Lippincott Co.

Kaiser, David. (2011). *How the Hippies Saved Physics.* New York: W.W. Norton & Company.

Kenniston, Kenneth. (1960). *Youth and Dissent: The Rise of New Opposition.* New York: Harcourt, Brace, Jovanovich, Inc.

Kesey, Ken. (1962) *One Flew Over The Cuckoo's Nest.* New York: Signet Books.

Kornbluth, Jesse (Ed.). (1968). *Notes from the New Underground.* New York: The Viking Press.

Lardas, M. (2001). *The Bop Apocalypse: The Religious Visions of Kerouac, Ginsberg, and Burroughs.* Chicago: University of Illinois Press.

Law, Lisa (2000). *Interviews with Icons.* Santa Fe: Lumen, Inc.

Markoff, John. (2005). *What The Dormouse Said.* New York: Penguin Books.

Mason, M. (2008). *The Pirate's Dilemma: How Youth Culture is Reinventing Capitalism.* NY: Free Press.

McCracken, Grant. (1988). *Culture and Consumption.* Bloomington: Indiana University Press.

Miller, Timothy. (1991). *The Hippies and American Values.* Knoxville: The University of Tennessee Press.

The *San Francisco Oracle,* Issues 1–12.

Perry, Charles. (2005). *The Haight-Ashbury: A History.* NY: Wenner Books.

Renzio, Toni del. (1968). *The Flower Children.* New York: Solstice Productions Ltd.

Rohé, Fred. (Working Paper). "ORGANIC FOR REAL: The Smart Food Movement," Transparency Market Research (April 2014).

Turner, Fred. (2008). *From Counterculture to Cyberculture Stewart Brand, The Whole Earth Network, and the Rise of Digital Utopianism.* Chicago: University of Chicago Press.

Westhues, Kenneth. (1972). *Society's Shadows: Studies in the Sociology of Countercultures.* New York: McGraw-Hill Ryerson Ltd.

Whitley, Lauren D. (2013) *Hippie Chic.* Boston: MFA Publications Museum of Fine Arts.

Williams, Reggie. *The Straight on the Haight.* Aurora, MO: Off the Wall Publications.

Wolfe, Burton. (1968). *The Hippies.* New York: Signet Books.

Wolfe, Tom (1968) *The Electric Kool-Aid Acid Test.* New York: Picador.

Yablonsky, Lewis. (1968). *The Hippie Trip.* New York: Pegasus.

INDEX

Note: References to photos and illustrations are printed in boldface type.